Shelton Publishing
2701 Weaver Hill Drive
Apex, NC 27502
www.coalmarch.com

Ordering Information:
Quantity sales. Special discounts are available on quantity purchases by corporations, associations, and others. For details, contact the publisher at the address above.

Publisher's Cataloging-in-Publication data
Shelton, Donnie.
The GROW! IMS : How to rapidly and profitably grow your service company online. / Donnie Shelton
p. cm.
Shelton Publishing
ISBN-13: 978-0692812365 (Custom Universal)
ISBN-10: 0692812369
1. Marketing. 2. Sales. 3. Business Development. 4. Inbound Marketing 5. Service Business Marketing

First Edition
1
Printed in the United States of America

TO EMILY CAROLINE
MAREN BLAKE AND
OWEN. YOU GUYS
INSPIRE ME TO BE THE
BEST THAT I CAN BE.

Contents

"Everyone has a plan 'till they get punched in the mouth."

- Mike Tyson

Introduction

Does This Sound Familiar?

Bob is scared. After reviewing his sales for the previous month, he notices that he has yet again failed to meet his sales goals, much less beat them. In fact, he not only missed his goal, he failed to match last year's sales for the same month. Bob knew that last month was not great, but he didn't realize it was this bad. Normally this would not be cause for concern, as Bob has seen ups and downs before. Those happen, he tells himself, and he could make up the difference this month or next. It's not the bad month that's scaring him, but the trend of more bad months than good, and his inability to get the phone ringing.

The reality is that Bob's company is dying a slow death. What has worked to get leads in the past no longer works. The direct mail, TV, radio, and yellow page sales people - and even his internet marketing agency - are telling him it will all turn around. But the fact is, Bob now faces competitors who are beating him online, taking up his market share, and even eating into his current customer base.

Bob doesn't understand online marketing very much. He knows he needs the internet to reach his target customers. He has hired countless SEO companies and self-proclaimed "experts," each of whom promised first-page results and more leads. But when Bob searches for his company on competitive keywords, he discovers that it's easier to find Waldo than it is to find his company online. Frustrated and defeated, Bob decides that maybe internet marketing is not for him. He doesn't understand it and apparently the "SEO experts" he has hired in the past don't either. Bob is in a vicious cycle, and he is stuck.

Just like Bob, Erin is scared. Unlike Bob, she has a very different problem. Her company is growing exponentially. Erin can't tell you exactly how fast it's growing because she doesn't have the time to critically analyze her key operating ratios. From the outside, Erin's business looks like a stunning success. She has outpaced all of her local competitors, and there are only two or three national companies that come close to matching her growth performance.

On the inside, her "stunning success" feels more like a stunning nightmare. Her company is growing so fast that she can't hire the right people fast enough. Most of her hires are made out of desperation, customer complaints are up, customer satisfaction scores are down, and her marketing and sales costs are through the roof.

Erin is using a marketing channel that works, but it is bleeding her dry. Her business is not generating a profit, and it hasn't for quite a long time. She is taking on debt to fund her growth. Her personal funds, credit lines and loans are all maxed out and she is not sure where to go to for more cash. She needs to grow more to pay her bills, but in order to grow more she has to pay even more money. Her growth is digging a hole that she's not quite sure she can climb out of. Erin is in a vicious cycle, and she is stuck.

My guess is that if you've been in business longer than 5 years you can probably identify, at least a little, with both Bob and Erin.

DO YOU MANAGE GROWTH OR DOES GROWTH MANAGE YOU?

As a service company, managing growth can be extremely difficult, especially if growth happens too fast or unexpectedly. Unlike product and commodity companies, you cannot scale and grow a service company easily.

The reason? Service companies require people.

A product company just needs to sell more product in order to grow. A service company, however, is a completely different story. When you grow a service company, you must hire and train more people. This, of course, takes time and comes with its own set of skills and challenges. Your capacity to satisfy customers must be aligned with your growth trajectory.

As a service company owner, if you can't properly manage your growth (meaning not too fast and not too slow) you will undoubtedly create a literal living hell. Grow too fast, and you will not be able to put the right people into the right seats, and your service will suffer. Grow too slowly and your "A" players will head for the exits when they see that there's no room for advancement.

The difference between an owner who knows how to manage growth versus an owner who doesn't comes down to one critical skill: The ability to grow rapidly AND profitably.

INBOUND MARKETING – THE SMART WAY TO GROW

There are two main types of marketing: inbound and outbound.

Outbound marketing is any type of marketing that interrupts the customer in order to offer a product or service. For example, the TV commercial during your favorite show, or the ad on Pandora that you've heard 100 times in the last two days, or the junk mail that you throw in the garbage every night without reading. In other words, it's annoying. So much so that customers are finding new ways to block these interruptions altogether, with inventions like ad blockers, email filters, commercial-skipping, and more.

That kind of inefficiency comes with a big cost. Your dollars aren't being spent on your target customer alone - they're being spent on a ton of people who aren't interested and may never be. It's like paying for a haystack just to get the needle.

In contrast, inbound marketing is truly targeted advertising. It is built to attract your ideal customer - someone with a demonstrated need for your service, who is ready to buy. This is exponentially more efficient and cost-effective, which means a healthier bottom line for your business.

THE GROW! INBOUND MARKETING SYSTEM™

Who I am

When I started my first service company, I was the technician, the accountant, the customer service rep, the marketing guy, and, of course, the manager. Yes, I've been in the trenches. I worked a lot of hours, & if there was a mistake to be made, I probably made it.

I have walked in both Bob's and Erin's shoes. I've had money issues, people issues, and customer issues. I know what it's like to grow too fast, I know what it's like to not grow fast enough. On more than one night, I have been up at 3am, worried about how I'll cover payroll. I've had employees leave when I needed them most. I've had customers not pay for our services.

In short, I'm not some "guru" or "consultant" who knows what you "should" be doing, but has never actually done it himself. I've lived the life of a service company owner and I continue to live it to this day. Even with all of its challenges, I love what I do. I am one of the lucky ones who turned something that I enjoy doing - growing companies - into a career. To me, there is nothing more fun than setting seemingly impossible goals and then crushing them.

One of the biggest lessons I have learned in the trenches is that the key to success in business (and in life) is to view almost everything that you do as a system. Once you view your business as one giant set of connected, smaller systems, all you need to do is standardize and perfect them for your business to become fun, easy, and chaos-free (mostly). Best of all, you won't be a slave to your business - your business will serve you.

This book focuses on the key system in your business that drives growth: marketing. It describes a system that will allow you to accomplish what most others believe is impossible: To grow fast and profitably. Most business owners believe that you can do one or the other, but not both at the same time. This is simply not true. With the Grow! IMS™ (Inbound Marketing System), your customer acquisition costs are a fraction of most other marketing channels', making the cost predictable, proven and profitable.

When I was growing my first service company, I had no investors and no cash reserves. I had to bootstrap my company and grow it on the money that I earned. I had to grow my company as fast and as cheaply as possible because I had no other options.

Though I would love to tell you otherwise, the truth is that the Grow! IMS™ was developed more out of sheer necessity than by any marketing genius.

With this marketing system, I have grown two service companies to the multi-million dollar level in less than four years. Keep in mind that, in my industry, it takes an average of about 10 years to reach the million dollar level. We did it with Grow! IMS™ in less than 4 years. I have also helped hundreds of other business owners grow their companies using this same system with comparable results. These companies range in sector, location, and size. The system gets results.

Why I decided to write this book

Since starting my first service company, countless other business owners have helped me immeasurably. The advice and knowledge that they shared with me has been literally worth millions of dollars. None of them ever asked for compensation, and all of them gave me their time and their advice freely. I will forever be grateful to these business owners and friends who helped me along the way. I would not be where I am today without them.

I wrote this book because I don't want you to go through what I did in order to grow your company. My hope is that this book does for you what others have done for me. While it is great to learn from your own experience, sometimes it is better to learn from the experience of others.

The Grow! IMS™ is the culmination of experiments that have worked and experiments that have spectacularly failed. Over time, and after a few embarrassments, I have refined this system and feel that it is ready to share with you. But knowledge is only part of the equation - executing it will be up to you.

You can grow rapidly and profitably

The Grow! IMS™ is designed to do one thing extremely well: to help you grow fast without being on the street corner collecting change. This system leverages a platform that generates the greatest possible number of customers at the lowest possible acquisition costs.

In other words, more money in for less money out.

If you are a service company that serves residential clients (B2C), I know that there is no better platform to acquire customers than inbound marketing. I have seen it work for companies large and small, in blue collar and white collar sectors, and in rural and urban markets.

This marketing system allows you to control your growth according to your goals. Whether you are a "steady as she goes" or a "blow the roof off" kind of business owner, the Grow! IMS™ allows the flexibility and predictability to accomplish your goals. It is the ultimate platform to put you in control of your revenue and profit growth depending on how fast you want to go.

Be warned though, if you are in the "blow the roof off" camp, then I do have a word of caution for you. A couple of years ago, I set up a good friend of mine on our marketing system, and his exact words were:

"Donnie, I want to grow. Give me everything. I want it to hurt! Don't hold back!"

I warned this business owner of the dangers of growing too fast, as it is very difficult to keep up with demand, but he insisted. A couple of months later he called me back with a different request.

"Donnie…. Uncle…. we need to slow down. I know what I said before, but we need to slow down".

Case in point? The Grow! IMS™ works VERY well. In some cases too well. As you begin to implement the system, take your time and go slow. Don't take a "no prisoners" approach to implementing the system, as it could backfire and you could be the one crying "uncle." Life is too short for that!

Grow! IMS™ - Your Inbound Playbook

If you want to grow faster, if you are growing but not making any money, or if you just can't seem to get any traction online, then the Grow! IMS™ is a time-tested, proven solution that can and will get you out of a rut. You don't have to be stuck any longer.

By using the Grow! IMS™, you will be one of the rare business owners who actually knows what you're doing online. You will spend your time and money on things that get results and let the other guys waste their money on mediocre marketing. You will be able to adjust your growth based on your goals and your capabilities. You will experience less stress, make more money, and make a positive impact on many people. Think about it, growing positively impacts your life - your team, your team's families, your customers, and, most importantly, your family. Kumbaya for everyone!

> **No matter what problems and challenges you are currently facing, there are very few problems that more sales cannot solve.**

So let's get to the business of learning how the Grow! IMS™ works and how to implement it into your company.

THIS BOOK HAS THREE SECTIONS:

Section 1

Section 1 is the foundation upon which the marketing system is built. It's how you develop the soil for implementing the Grow! IMS™ system. It's about fortifying your company so you can extract the maximum value from your investment of time and money. Without mastering the fundamentals of your marketing, any time spent online will be an utter waste of time and money. Stephen R. Covey once famously said, "The main thing is to keep the main thing the main thing". Consider Section 1 of the book "the main thing" of the Grow! IMS™.

Section 2

Section 2 is the brass tacks of the marketing system. I show you how to organize your messaging, brand, and platforms so that you are able to connect with your customers in a meaningful way. I also show you how to create an online strategy that gets results, not a bunch of hope and change.

Section 3

Section 3 guides you through implementing the system. It shows you how to best execute the system and how to hire an inbound team that is more interested in your success than your wallet.

"Only those who will risk going too far can possibly find out how far one can go."

- T.S. Eliot

Chapter 1

Grow! Fast
Grow! Profitably

A few years ago, in late December, I was returning to Raleigh from a business trip in Detroit on a seemingly routine Southwest flight. I was tired, ready to be back home with my family, and I ended up sleeping most of the flight. As the plane landed and we began taxiing to the terminal, something happened that I will never forget.

The flight attendant picked up the microphone and started singing "We Wish You a Merry Christmas." At first, it was just her singing. She didn't have the best voice, but her enthusiasm was contagious. She sang the entire first verse smiling and with feeling and as the passengers looked from her to each other, they began smiling too. As she ended the first verse, she exclaimed, "Now everyone! We wish you a merry Christmas, we wish you a merry Christmas…"

Needless to say, the entire plane sang along - loudly and in harmony. When we all finished, everyone began clapping, and I sat there absolutely amazed at how just a few seconds earlier I was tired, weary, and ready to get home. Now, after singing a song with the flight attendant and all of my fellow passengers, I was elated. I was happy and in the holiday spirit. As we exited the airplane, most of the passengers thanked the flight attendant and some even hugged her. Like I said, this seemingly small, unexpected act was an experience I will never forget.

I was and still am a loyal Southwest Airlines customer. I don't always fly on their airline, but they are my first choice any time I need to travel in the United States. If a flight of theirs fits my schedule and location, I take it.

As it turns out, my story and experience on Southwest is not unique. They are known to have funny, friendly, and hard-working employees. There are countless stories of Southwest employees singing songs, rapping the safety briefing, and in general using humor to make flying on their airline fun and exciting.

Southwest's amazing customer experience, and their culture, and their humour, and their reputation is something that other airlines can't even begin to replicate. In its 50 years of operation, they've NEVER had an unprofitable quarter. In an industry known for stacking up massive losses, Southwest has managed to turn a profit every single year and every single quarter. Even after September 11th, they managed to turn a profit. In fact, after that horrendous day, customers were so concerned for the well-being of the company that they sent checks and personal letters wishing them well.

Southwest is an interesting company because it is so different than its competitors. They don't have first class, there is no assigned seating, they only fly B-737s, and they have the highest customer service satisfaction rating of any airline.

In his wonderful book, *Built to Last*, Jim Collins discusses a key finding that is common among all great companies and absent from their counterparts: great companies "embrace the and." Great companies have a core ideology that guides them and their decision making, but they understand that they also must grow. Truly great companies are able to stimulate change and preserve their core simultaneously.

You can see the validity of this concept from your own experience. What company do you enjoy doing business with the most? Why? I enjoy doing business with Southwest Airlines because they are usually on time, and their employees are fun, and I don't have to wait on the "triple-double platinum, gold, silver medallion status" passengers to board, and their fares are usually cheaper and... you get the idea.

GROWTH - CONVENTIONAL WISDOM

Conventional wisdom does not "embrace and." In fact, conventional wisdom actually breeds mediocrity by embracing the "or."

High Growth Conventional Wisdom

Conventional wisdom states that companies that are in high growth mode should grow revenue and market share at all costs. The thought process goes something like this:

> **A company should grow market share as fast and as quickly as possible, without regard for profit.**

If you look at most startups and high growth companies today, you will see that this is their continual mantra. It is not uncommon for a company to lose money for years before turning a profit. The battlefield of business is littered with companies gone bust from using this growth strategy.

While it is true that you can grow a company extremely fast on debt and investment money, this is far from a sound business strategy. The majority of business owners don't have a cache of investment dollars to fund that kind of growth. There are other limitations with this strategy as well. When you are growing this fast, it is all but impossible to put the right people into the right seats. Instead of creating a great and strong company, you end up creating a bozo magnet company. What does that mean? It means you hire a bozo because you need a body, and the bozo attracts more bozos to your business and so begins your path to mediocrity.

Low Growth Conventional Wisdom

Conventional wisdom states that companies that are in low growth mode should preserve profit at all costs. The thought process goes something like this:

A company should take little if any risks to preserve profit.

Do you know how to spot a business owner who is completely disengaged and ready to sell? Look for extremely high profit. While it is important to have cash reserves and avoid unnecessary risks, not growing can kill you too. Think about it. As the internet was gaining in popularity, the Yellow Pages absolutely owned all marketing associated with local service companies. Who was best positioned to take advantage of this new technology? Who had a ton of cash? At the time, the Yellow Pages was an absolute cash cow. Each year the business kicked off with more than 300% profit. Instead of investing those profits in building the infrastructure for the next generation of advertising, executives decided to implement the FDH strategy: Fat, Dumb, and Happy.

Lack of rapid growth tends to breed complacency in you & in your team. High growth offers challenges and opportunities for you &

your team, and ensures the long-term viability of your company.

GROWTH - UNCONVENTIONAL WISDOM

At the core of these "conventional wisdoms" is the choice to pursue high growth or high profit, but not both. It is the proverbial "embracing the or."

I am here to tell you that conventional wisdom is dead wrong. It is possible to have high growth and high profit at the same time. There are companies such as Southwest Airlines, Chick-Fil-A, Zappos, and Amazon who are disproving this "embrace the or" concept each and every day.

If you take nothing else from this chapter, take this:

High growth and high profit is the best business strategy.

Embracing the "and" of high growth and high profit as a business strategy is the key to growing a great and enduring organization. When you embrace a high-growth strategy, it forces you and your company to stay lean and mean, with a focus on the future and the discipline to look for and develop new opportunities.

In 2009, when the market melted down from the subprime mortgage loan crisis, automakers flocked to Washington, D.C. for a handout to save their businesses.

For years, the auto industry paid higher than average salaries and promised extremely generous retirement packages for all their workers. Everyone from the janitor to the CEO was well-compensated, and when the storm came, none of them were prepared to weather it. None of them with the exception of Ford.

By 2009, Ford's CEO Alan Mulally was well into his strategy of generating high profitability for Ford. When the crisis hit the auto industry, Ford took no bailout money from the government because it simply didn't need it. The previous profitable months leading up to the crisis provided the cash reserves needed to weather the storm. Ford's already efficient operations were able to generate profit despite a downturn in automobile sales.

By embracing the "and" of revenue and profit growth, your company positions itself for the long-term while being prepared for the storms as they come in. Plus, it is much less stressful and enjoyable to be a part of a company that is so prepared.

While conventional wisdom believes that it is not possible to have high growth and high profit at the same time, it is possible. The keys are:

- Ensure that your services are appropriately priced to provide an adequate profit margin.
- Ensure that your customer acquisition costs are low.

INBOUND MARKETING - THE PATH TO EMBRACING THE "AND"

One of the biggest challenges of a high growth focused company is to self-fund its own growth. Usually this is due to high customer acquisition costs. Too frequently, growing companies get themselves into trouble by "growing broke." That is, they grow at any expense (and even go into debt) to continue growth. While that strategy may be sexy on Wall Street, on Main Street it is a recipe for disaster. There are no investors that will bail you out and you're not "too big to fail." If you need validation of this, just miss a loan payment and see how your banker handles the situation.

Inbound marketing is arguably the best method to grow your service company, period! No other marketing channel comes even remotely close when evaluated on the criteria of volume and low customer acquisition costs.

Inbound marketing is the bedrock to "embrace the and" to grow your company fast and profitably. It's the difference between buying your clothes at Wal-Mart versus buying them at Gucci. In both cases, the clothing functions the same (it covers your body) but your acquisition costs are VERY different.

Inbound marketing gives you the ability to market to your target demographic, in your target location, to people who are interested in and ready to buy your service, all at a fraction of the cost of most other traditional marketing methods.

Another major benefit is flexibility. In my business, we've noticed a curious phenomenon: every summer, when we're running at 110% and our schedule is packed to the max, a tech gets sick, or gets in an accident, or decides to leave the business. Of course, it's at that exact moment that sales shoot through the roof. At this point, we have a running joke that, if sales are dipping, someone needs to get sick to reverse the trend.

With inbound marketing, you have the flexibility to go as fast or as slow as you like. There are limitations based on demand, of course (for those of you who want to go super fast,) but if you find yourself in a bind, you have the ability to slow down the lead flow in a matter of seconds.

The point here is that if you want to "embrace the and" to create a company like Southwest Airlines, where you provide a phenomenal customer experience and you have phenomenal growth and you have phenomenal profit, there is no better vehicle than inbound marketing to get you there. With inbound marketing you can generate the high volume of leads that you need to grow fast while at the same time keeping your customer acquisition costs low. Hence you can grow fast and you can grow profitably.

Before describing the entire inbound system in Part II, the next two chapters will address your mindset and whether your company is ready to grow. Think of these as a pre-flight check before you begin rapid, profitable growth.

CHAPTER SUMMARY & ACTION CHECKLIST

- Conventional wisdom is dead wrong and will not give you the results you desire. Great companies reject the idea that you can only have high growth or high profit. Great companies embrace the "and" by growing fast and growing profitably.

- High growth and high profit is not only possible, but your best business strategy. High growth prevents complacency and reduces your risk while you are growing.

- Inbound marketing is the ultimate platform for high growth and high profit. With inbound marketing you acquire a high volume of customers at very low acquisition costs.

"He that is good for making excuses is seldom good for anything else."

- Benjamin Franklin

Chapter 2

Are You Ready to Grow!?

It has been said that in business, timing is everything. At 30 years old I was on top of the world. I had just been accepted to Duke's prestigious MBA program, I was a pilot in the United States Air Force Reserve, and I was a lead software developer for a Fortune 500 company. Everything in my life was going great...until I decided to start my own service company.

My timing could not have been worse. My wife was a stay-at-home mom with a newborn and a 3-year-old. Striking out on my own in a service industry that I knew nothing about was a huge risk, and the consequences for failure were potentially catastrophic. So, I did what any illogical person would do. I quit my day job and turned down the opportunity to earn the MBA.

Six months into this decision, I was failing miserably. I was burning cash like it was my job, my employees were running all over me, and I couldn't keep up with the demands of my customers. Worst of all, the pressure to provide for my family was overwhelming. If I continued down the path I was on, failure was all but guaranteed.

Seeing the writing on the wall, I decided to attend a leadership conference sponsored by our industry association. I had a lot to learn and I knew it. But I resolved to be totally engaged with both the speakers and the most successful owners at that meeting.

Right from the start, I followed through on this commitment. I introduced myself to all the speakers and to all of the successful owners, I furiously took notes, and made action plans to implement much-needed changes. Most importantly, I made a commitment to myself in that meeting that I would do whatever it takes to be successful. No amount of hours, work, or money was going to stop me. I was not going to fail. That decision, to totally and completely engage in my business at all costs, was one of the best business decisions I've ever made.

During the conference proceedings, I could not help but notice a 2nd generation business owner in front of me. He had just been given the reigns of a successful service company that his dad started over 30 years earlier. His dad started the company with nothing and grew it based on great customer service and excellent management.

The 2nd generation owner was about the same age as I was when we attended the conference. I wondered if he was feeling some of the same pressures that I was feeling. Surely he had to be concerned about continuing his father's legacy.

With the new responsibilities and the pressure to build on what his father started, how engaged do you think he was during the presentations? Was he taking notes and planning his next move as a business owner? Was he recording his impressions and the ideas he generated as the speakers presented? Was he figuring out how to take his business to the next level, taking advantage of the resources and staff his dad never had?

Nope.

He wasn't doing any of that.

As the first speaker began her presentation, this business owner simply pulled out his laptop and started browsing bass boat websites. This was appalling to me, but what really astounded me was that he chose bass boats over fully engaging in the content of the meeting for the entire two days of the conference.

There I was, literally living hand to mouth to support my family, and this guy with all the opportunity in the world - money, management, systems, and a dad to coach him - was squandering an opportunity that wound up giving me a lifetime of valuable knowledge.

Fast-forward 10 years and the numbers tell the story of owner engagement. This 2nd generation business owner operates a successful service company. In fact, he has managed to grow his business roughly 5-8% every year since that meeting. By normal industry standards he would be considered successful.

Meanwhile, my company, which has been in business for 10 years, has grown to over twice the size of his, which has been in operation for over 40 years. I tell this story not to glorify my success or diminish his, but to provide an example that highlights a very important question that must be answered.

What made the difference in his growth versus mine?

We both offer the same service in the same market, so we have equal opportunity. He had a definite advantage 10 years ago, as he was building on a well-established brand and company, while I was just starting out.

So what made the difference? Was it marketing? Maybe it was management. What about key people?

The answer is: all of the above. We out-marketed, out-recruited, and out-serviced him, just as we did a lot of things way better than all of our competitors. But that's not what explains the difference in growth and profit 10 years later. What explains the difference is much, much deeper than a specific strategy.

ENGAGEMENT - THE GROW! IMS™ KEYSTONE

In architectural design, the arch is known for both its beauty and its utility. Architects often use the arch in building design due to the uniqueness of its structure and its ability to withstand incredible loads with a minimal amount of material.

Masonry arches do not naturally occur in nature. Its construction is made possible only by two components:

- **Springers** - The stones on which the arch rests
- **Keystone** - The center stone that locks all other stones into place

While all the stones of the arch are important, it is the keystone alone that enables the structure to bear weight.

As we examine the Grow! IMS™ and we review all of the individual components of the system, there is one concept that I want you keep in mind throughout the building process.

ENGAGEMENT IS THE KEYSTONE OF THE GROW! IMS™

In a service company, what makes a company more successful than its peers?

Is it better products? Better marketing? Better technology? Better cost structure? Research and experience shows that it's actually none of these. While all of these elements are important and contribute to the success of any successful service company, they don't get to the root of the real reason for success. All of these elements can be copied over time and none of them alone offer a long-term competitive advantage.

Empirically, research study after research study shows that the key differentiator in creating a sustainable competitive business advantage are the people who work in the company. Your people, the ones who actually do the work, provide the ONLY long-term competitive advantage that you have. Digging into the research further, the key to teams outperforming their peers is clear:

Companies with fully engaged employees significantly outperform their peers.

What does it mean to be engaged? Clearly stated, a fully engaged employee is motivated to contribute to the organization's success and is willing to apply themselves in whatever way it takes to achieve that end - overtime, extra brain power, personal development, etc…

In the service industry, the idea of engagement as a key differentiator is even more important because your business depends exclusively on the people providing the service. We all have the same products, same marketing, same procedures, and the same people.

As it turns out, the keystone of the Grow! IMS™ has nothing to do with marketing at all. Indeed, the keystone of the Grow! IMS™ is high employee engagement. Growing your company both rapidly and profitability is all about engagement first, then executing on your strategy.

Before you implement - look in the mirror

Michael Gerber, the author of the E-Myth™ series, said something that I have never forgotten regarding engagement. He said, in effect, "show me a small business owner, then give me a mirror and I'll show you what their business looks like."

Think about it. Have you ever observed this phenomenon? I have. I know some small business owners who handle their frustrations by unloading on people when they're angry. They bully and belittle their managers, and guess what those managers do to their direct reports? Other owners cheat their employees by not paying a fair wage or not paying for worked time. How do you think their employees handle opportunities to cheat back?

On the other hand, I have small business owner friends whose businesses are a shining example of their character and work ethic. My dentist, whom I have used for over 20 years, has the kindest staff that I've ever met. His turnover is almost non-existent and his business is highly successful. Can you guess the personality and engagement level of this owner?

The point here is, like it or not, your business is a reflection of you. Research shows time after time that when people aren't quite sure how to behave, they look to others in the same situation to figure it out. When you hire new employees, they look to your current employees to figure what your culture is like and how they should behave. Your current employees look to you - the owner, the leader - for how to behave.

Can a disengaged leader create a company of engaged employees?

The answer to this question is very obvious, but you should take some time to really think about what your employees are mirroring from you. Are you modeling the exact same behaviors you want them to exhibit? What are you engaged in? Are you consumed with other interests (like bass boats) rather than rapidly and profitably growing your company?

Going back to the question of identifying the key differentiator between me and the bass boat owner, the answer is emphatically - engagement!

If you can assemble a team of engaged employees, that team will find a way to succeed in any circumstance. They will learn, they will push, they will execute, and they will persevere. Getting your team engaged is not easy, but it is impossible if you are not engaged in high profitable growth yourself.

Set your keystone

Many years ago, a young man who wanted to obtain wisdom decided to ask one of the wisest men of his age, Aristotle, a simple question. "How can I have wisdom?" Unmoved by this young man's question, Aristotle calmly replied, "follow me".

The young man followed Aristotle down several streets through their town until they finally reached a shallow pool in the city square. Without any warning, Aristotle (a man large in stature) grabbed the young man and held his head underwater. The young man struggled, flailed, and fought Aristotle for air, all to no avail. Aristotle was simply too strong. Waiting for what must have seemed like an eternity to the young man, Aristotle finally pulled him out of the water and dragged him to the edge of the pool.

Aristotle then asked the puzzled young man (who was gasping for air) a simple yet subtle question. "Young man, when I held you under water, what did you want more than anything in this world?" Without hesitation, the young man responded "air." Aristotle then answered the young man's original question. "Only when you want wisdom as badly as you just wanted air, will you find it".

Just like the young man, who desperately wanted air as Aristotle held him underwater, you must feel that same intensity for rapid, profitable growth. Total and complete engagement is the air that makes it happen.

Engagement is overcoming fears and committing to continual learning of new ways to grow your company. Engagement is listening and taking notes in conferences so that you can remember the most valuable information and put it to use in your company. Engagement is focusing on results and not excuses for mediocrity.

In short, engagement is the absolute commitment on your part to do whatever is necessary to grow your company and be successful.

The keystone of the Grow! IMS™ is your engagement. It takes committed, highly engaged leaders to rapidly and profitably grow a service company. It takes your total engagement to lead your people to full engagement. Anything less will result in slow or no growth and limited profits.

Once you've committed to being 100% engaged in the business of rapidly and profitably growing your service company, it's time for one more final pre-flight check before jumping into the strategy of the Grow! IMS™.

CHAPTER SUMMARY & ACTION CHECKLIST

- Engagement is the cornerstone to The Grow! IMS™. Without it, you will not succeed. Don't be a "bass boat" owner when it comes to growing your business.

- Engagement begins with you. The company is a reflection of you. Leading a company implies that you are in front and people are following you.

- A company with fully engaged employees significantly outperforms its peers.

"There is only one boss. The customer. And he can fire everybody in the company from the chairman on down, simply by spending his money somewhere else."

- Sam Walton

Chapter 3

Is Your Company Ready to Grow!?

A couple of years ago, I decided to surprise my wife with a cruise to the Bahamas for our fifteen year anniversary. Preparing and planning for the surprise trip was straightforward. All I needed to plan were our flights to Port Canaveral, our cab rides to and from the ship, and for the grandparents to watch our kids while we were away.

When the big day arrived, everything was going as planned. The grandparents showed up on time and I became an instant hero and celebrity when my wife figured out what I had done.

The cab to the ship arrived a little late, but I didn't mind as I had plenty of time built into the schedule so we weren't in a rush. The friction point came once we got into the cab. It was beat up and dirty, with three hubcaps, seats that looked as if they'd been ravaged by a lion, and it reeked of smoke.

Luckily, my wife is pretty low-maintenance. Despite the less than ideal situation, we dealt with the 1st world problems of the cab as we drove to the cruise ship. During the ride, the driver offered what I considered good customer service. He made small talk, was very courteous when speaking to my wife and me, and he handled our luggage with care.

While we did get to the port and the driver was nice, we were both nauseated from the cigarette smoke in the cab by the time we got to the ship. Our clothing also reeked of cigarette smoke. We paid a premium price for the ride, and my wife, who is way nicer than me, felt obligated to leave the driver a generous tip despite our nausea, because he talked with us as he drove us to the ship.

Looking back on this experience, I'd say that the company offered good customer service but not a good customer experience.

What a difference a few months and a smartphone makes

Fast forward only a few months. I attended a conference in Seattle and I needed to get from the airport to the conference center located downtown. Once I'd landed, I pulled out my smartphone, opened the Uber app, and with one click arranged for transportation to the conference center. The app showed me a picture of the driver, what other customers thought of him, the make and model of the car, and his license plate number so that I could easily identify him. It also gave me his present location along with his estimated arrival time.

As I passed the line of cabs waiting in vain for riders, I couldn't help but think of how badly the cab industry must be hurting. This was the first time that I have ever seen a line of cabs waiting for customers that simply were not there.

As I arrived at the Uber waiting area, I could barely find a place to stand because there were so many people waiting for their Uber rides. Suddenly my phone buzzed to let me know that my driver had arrived.

The driver was very kind, he took great care of my luggage, and best of all his car was clean and modern. As we drove to the conference center, the driver was courteous and made sure to tell me about a few things I should do in the city. Once at the conference center, I simply got out of the car, got my luggage, and walked off. No waiting for a credit card machine to charge my card, no awkward moments of determining a tip, and most importantly, no shower after the ride. I even got an email receipt just after the ride with an invitation to rate the driver.

In just a few months from my experience in Port Canaveral to my experience in Seattle, Uber entered the cab market and completely turned the industry upside down.

The cab industry has been around since the 17th century, and back then the concept of a cab was a revolution for customers. That was over 400 years ago, and it took apps like Uber and Lyft to shake things up.

Now instead of waiting on an unreliable, possibly dirty, and expensive cab with an unsafe driver who talks on his cell phone while driving 20 miles over the speed limit, you can whip out your smartphone and, with one click, arrange for transportation without any worrying about what the cab is going to look like, how much you are going to tip, or if the driver will even show up. You will rate the driver, and the driver will rate you. It's an easy and transparent experience, and the entire process is truly a customer-centric process.

So how did small startups like Uber and Lyft manage to completely uphend a 400-year-old service business model? How is it that in a matter of months the cab companies went from making the rules to asking for governmental intervention to save their businesses? How is it that this industry failed to see or capitalize on this massive opportunity? Some would point to technology, while others would blame regulators, but the reality is that the answer is much, much deeper than that.

Your customer has changed

Caroline is the epitome of a busy and productive person. The demands on her time with appointments and commitments are overwhelming and yet somehow she miraculously manages to get it all done. Caroline is highly educated and has disposable income.

She is very willing to use that disposable income on products or services that do one very important thing: save her time. She's even willing to pay more, as long as they don't rob her of that precious commodity.

Caroline has high expectations. She is accustomed to companies who understand her and put her at the center of their universe. Companies like Zappos and Amazon make it easy for her to get things done on the go, and they know her preferences and her likes. She feels these companies just "get" her and her crazy life.

Caroline is always on, always connected, and highly opinionated. She has a voice that is loud and far reaching. She knows that she is part of a larger conversation with other consumers concerning a company's service. She is not afraid to tell others what she thinks of a company, whether it's good or bad. She's not looking to do harm, but look out if you cross her.

Caroline has the power of choice, and she knows it. In the past, her parents and grandparents only had one, maybe two, choices when it came to consuming products and services. For Caroline, that number is in the hundreds of thousands. In a matter of seconds, Caroline can access a trove of data on all of her options and then rack and stack companies based on past customer experiences. She is very adept at researching products and services and she never makes a purchase without researching first. If a business doesn't have a track record providing a great customer experience, she simply moves on to a company that does.

Ultimately, Caroline wants to do business with a company that she can trust to give her a great experience, not just a product or service. An experience that not only gives her what she needs, but also ensures that she can protect her time. She knows that a company focused on her experience will "embrace the and." That is to say, a CX (customer experience) company that Caroline does business with provides her a product or service and respects her time.

It's not customer service, it's CX

So how is it that companies like Uber, Lyft, and Amazon can upend industries in a matter of months? It's that they get this one simple idea:

It's the total CX, not just customer service that matters.

Customer experience is the total interaction between an organization and a customer over the duration of their relationship. All interactions with the customer are part of the CX, including building awareness, attraction, cultivation, and ultimately, the use of a service. In other words, your service works, it's easy to use, and you're fast.

Companies like Amazon and Uber understand that customers are not willing to suffer through bad experiences any longer. These companies are interested in each of the interactions they have with a customer, and how those interactions can create a long-term relationship. Amazon and Uber view their service as an experience, not just a service.

Customer experience encompasses more than simple customer service. It is entirely possible for a company to offer phenomenal customer service, while at the same time providing a poor customer experience. The cab that took my wife and me to the cruise ship had great customer service, but I would never use them again because the experience was poor. Companies like Uber and Lyft understood my common frustration, "embraced the and," and created a completely new and better experience.

CX FIRST, THEN GROW! IMS™

What is the CX like now at your company? What empirical data can you reference to validate your answer?

The reality is that most service company owners and managers have no idea what their CX really is. Oftentimes, especially in service businesses, owners make a critical mistake in thinking that if their service is good, customers will use their company. Ask the cab companies across America how that strategy is working out for them.

In order to attract customers like Caroline and to build loyalty to your brand, you have to understand that your CX is the foundation for success in your sales and marketing efforts. Without a great

CX, your company will struggle, and, just like the cab company, will be upended by companies that focus on the entire CX.

If you don't know what your CX is, then commit to measuring and ultimately improving it. While there are several great books that cover this topic extensively, let's cover three basic things that you can do to improve CX immediately:

- **Identify and Eliminate Friction Points** - Look for things that customers don't like to do or things that make a customer wait. Starting points for a service company would be hold times, call to service time, and the time to take a specific action on your website.

- **Be Transparent** - Look for ways to keep your customers constantly informed. Starting points for a service company include who the service professional will be, what time they will arrive, how long the appointment will last, and what to expect.

- **Use Feedback** - Make it super easy for your customers to let you know how you're doing. For a service company, this includes after-service emails and quality service phone calls.

Ultimately, understanding what your CX is and committing to constantly improving it will be the key to creating and maintaining long-term relationships with customers. CX is truly your path to rapid, profitable growth.

ONE BIG ASSUMPTION

Have you ever been in stop-and-go traffic when you see the dirtbag on the right shoulder passing everyone because he is "more special" than everyone else? I have seen state troopers give these folks tickets and I have seen other drivers block out the right-shoulder cheaters by straddling the lane and the shoulder. The reality is that no one likes people who think they can shortcut the drive while everyone else waits for traffic to move.

No one likes these people, including your customers.

While many people try, there really are no shortcuts to rapid, profitable growth. Some "right shoulder" business owners believe, foolishly, that they can skip the hard work of creating a phenomenal CX and just hire a marketing company to drive and manage their growth.

When marketing is done right, it can be a powerful tool to grow your business. However, if you want to become a great company, you cannot jump on the shoulder of the road and bypass CX. The idea that a marketing team can grow a company with a bad CX is akin to believing in the Tooth Fairy or Santa Claus.

In this new world of the always-connected, always-on, highly opinionated customer, this will surely backfire. If you try to "right shoulder" CX and go straight to implementing the Grow! IMS™, customers will revolt and ultimately give your company an online presence that looks more like a Lindsay Lohan rap sheet than a reputable service company worthy of a potential customer's money.

One very big assumption that the Grow! IMS™ makes is that you have a good customer experience. It does not have to be perfect, but it does have to be good. At a minimum, before implementing the Grow! IMS, your company should be able to make and keep your promises to your customers. If you tell a customer that you are going to be there at 9AM, you'd better be able to execute that promise consistently.

Assuming that you can keep your promises and that your CX is where it needs to be, then we are all done with the pre-flight checks and are now ready to get started with the Grow! IMS.

In the next section we are going to go through each component of the Grow! IMS™. I will show you how each step works, explain why it works, and then show you how to implement that step. I think you will find, as many others have, that fast, profitable growth is easy and fun if you do it right.

CHAPTER SUMMARY & ACTION CHECKLIST

- Your customer has changed in the internet age. Your customers buy time and care about the total experience with your company, not just the quality.

- It's the total customer experience (CX) that matters today, not just customer service. Make sure that all areas of your service company are focused on making it easy for the customer.

- You must focus on your CX first and get it consistently excellent before implementing The GROW! IMS™. Building your company online with a bad CX will backfire and do more damage than good.

"Winning is habit. Unfortunately, so is losing."

- Vince Lombardi

Chapter 4

The Grow! IMS ™ Overview

The United States Air Force is an absolutely amazing organization when you think about it. At any given time, in all parts of the world, there are aircraft with aircrew flying missions 24 hours a day, 365 days a year - 366 on leap years. These missions involve transport, surveillance, refueling, bombing, and air-to-air fighting. Some of these missions are training, some are operational, while others happen in actual combat.

Take just a moment to grasp how complex it is to maintain an air platform all across the world. There are time zone issues, there are country-specific issues, there are aircraft issues, there are maintenance issues, there are pilot training issues, there are medical issues, there are mission issues, and the list goes on and on.

There are literally thousands of aircraft located in hundreds of locations. The number of aircraft change everyday, the locations those aircraft operate in change every hour, and the people who must operate those aircraft change every single hour, too. There is no such thing as a day off, and the mission never stops.

Each part of the air platform has its own set of unique needs that must be managed on a daily basis. The aircraft must get fueled, the pilots must be trained, the missions must be coordinated with other countries, etc, etc… and yet the Air Force manages to consistently fulfill its mission successfully on a global scale.

I've flown in the Air Force reserve for over a decade and I've had the privilege of being a part of this highly complex and highly effective organization. I joined the Air Force when I was 17; my mother had to sign me in because I was not old enough to sign a contract. Joining this organization turned out to be one of the best life and business decisions I have ever made, as it taught me both the value and effectiveness of standards and systems.

Once a member of the Air Force, you realize very quickly that the organization itself is highly reliant on standardization and systems. It has to be. How else can you employ aircraft, aircrew, support personnel, parts, etc, on a global scale and keep up with it all? By what other means could so many moving parts be coordinated to carry out the mission of the Air Force so consistently and effectively?

As a pilot, I am dependent on systems, standards and checklists when I am in the air. When flying, there are countless life or death decisions that must be made quickly and correctly. The systems, standards and checklists all work together to provide a structure that ensures that the majority of my decisions will be accurate and the best method to address the given situation. I have procedures for starting engines and for shutting them down. I have standards for how to land the airplane, to judge if an approach is good and whether or not to take an aircraft airborne. In short, the number of standards and procedures that I must know feel like the equivalent of having to know and understand all of the articles on Wikipedia.

Although Hollywood would like for you to believe that a good pilot has "the right stuff" and "is a loose cannon", most pilots will tell you that the great pilots are the ones that know their systems, procedures and checklists extremely well. Indeed, the vast majority of aircraft accidents attributed to human error are almost always a result of a pilot not following these guidelines. Likewise, in just about every heroic recovery of a disabled aircraft you will find that the pilot followed the system to safely land the aircraft.

THE VALUE OF USING A STRUCTURED SYSTEM

So what exactly is a system? More importantly, what do systems have to do with marketing? Isn't marketing supposed to be about creativity and "outside the box" thinking?

Michael Gerber, the author of the E-Myth™ book series, gave one of the clearest definitions of a system that I have ever read. He states:

> *"A system is a set of things, actions, ideas, and information that interact with each other, and in so doing, alter other systems"*

This means that, in reality, everything is a system. The Air Force, your company, your family, the way you tie your shoes, the way you brush your teeth, and so on and so forth. Whether we are aware of them or not, in the real world we use systems every day to provide predictable, consistent, and effective results.

A system doesn't have to be complicated or confusing. A system just needs to have the following 4 basic components:

- **Procedures** - A system must have a structured approach to provide a specific result. Procedures provide both the "how to" aspect of the system along with the order. If your system has no procedures and no order, then it is not a system at all. Procedures allow the system to be performed in a manner that produces consistent, repeatable results.

- **Reliable Result** - A system must provide a reliable, desired result. If the system cannot produce your desired result consistently then you either don't have a system, or you have a broken one. In either case, it is time to go back to the drawing board.

- **Quantification** - A system must be quantifiable to indicate if you achieved your objective or not. With quantification you can evaluate the effectiveness of your system along with the effects that system modifications have on desired results.

- **Standards** - Any system must have performance standards. The idea is that, with standards, there is a common way to approach problems and tasks. The real value from standards is the ability to improve. Standards allow you to test new ideas, methods and technologies in your system and empirically validate the effectiveness of the change.

Systems, standards, and procedures provide a structure to help you provide effective, consistent and phenomenal results. Once you have identified a quantifiable desired result, all that is needed are standards and procedures, and you have a system.

SUCCESSFUL ORGANIZATIONS USE SYSTEMS

All highly effective people and organizations are big into systems. They understand the need to be consistently great, and they don't believe in winging it to possibly get the desired result.

Can you imagine an Air Force where they just winged it when it came to training a pilot? What if they winged it to figure out what parts they should keep on base? Pilots would be flying aircraft into the ground, and of the aircraft left, none would get off of the ground because they'd be broken.

The marketing of your company is a system. There are growth targets that you must achieve (quantification), procedures that ensure that result, a reliable way to produce that result and best practices (standards) that help you avoid making mistakes and optimize your efforts.

THE GROW! IMS SYSTEM™

At its core, the Grow! IMS™ is a simple yet comprehensive system. I developed and perfected this system over the years of growing my service company and the service companies of my customers. The Grow! IMS™ is a set of procedures, standards and checklists that provide your business with a consistent, reliable and quantifiable source of leads and sales that can help you grow your business.

The Grow! IMS has been validated in multiple service industries,

in multiple markets, and with multiple demographics. It works for small companies, it works for multi-million dollar companies. Simply stated, if you own a service company, the Grow! IMS™ provides a structure for reliable and consistent growth at whatever rate you choose to grow.

This system is designed for service company owners.

Before we dive into all of the components of the system, there is one very important point I want to make: The Grow! IMS™ is designed for service company business owners.

You don't need to be a tech guru or an internet dynamo in order to reap the benefits of this system. The Grow! IMS™ provides the mindset, structure and overall approach to build an inbound marketing strategy that will achieve your growth and profit goals. The system does not explain all the technical aspects of inbound marketing, as most business owners have neither the skill nor the time to spend on technical details. In addition, written instructions on the technical aspects quickly become outdated, as changes occur almost weekly.

DON'T STRAY FROM THE SYSTEM

Have you ever been to a party and there's a guy there who seemingly knows everything there is to know about tech stuff? You can sniff out these guys a mile away because they all seem to have some common traits:

- They have the latest smartphone.
- They work in a technical field that involves computers .
- They use words that you've never heard of and make jokes about things you've never heard of.

While I don't want you to deflate anyone's ego and I don't want to be responsible for a fight, resist the temptation of listening to these guys. I'm not saying that some of them don't have great advice. But when they pontificate about the particulars of technology and then offer you suggestions on what you "should" be doing to grow your business, exercise caution.

Each step in the Grow! IMS™ is designed specifically for service companies, and it has been validated. While some technology and new developments are indeed awesome, that doesn't mean that it will be a good fit for your service business. For example, years ago I decided that I needed to go big on social media because I attended a conference where a speaker extolled the "magic" of Facebook contests. I came back from the conference both determined and excited. After giving away 10 iPads with no sales to show for them, I realized one hard truth: no one wants to connect with a pest control company on Facebook.

The point is: don't assume just because something works for someone else or in another industry that it will automatically work for you and your industry. I'm not saying don't experiment, but if you start experimenting and changing key parts of the system, you run the risk of getting poor and inconsistent results.

ORDER IS IMPORTANT

The Grow! IMS™ is divided into 3 major phases, and the order is important.

Phase 1 - Covers the foundation of all of your marketing. In this phase of the system, we establish clarity and organization in your marketing so that you can maximize your results in the next two phases.

Phase 2- Covers your overall conversion strategy. The idea is to completely and totally maximize every opportunity to get people to take an action on your website.

Phase 3 - Covers how to get the maximum amount of traffic to your website with the highest possible efficiency (e.g. lowest costs).

These phases should be done in order, and all items in each phase should be completed before moving to the next phase. If you decide not to follow the order or not complete an entire phase, you will most certainly lose money.

Oftentimes business owners approach their marketing in the exact opposite order of the Grow! IMS™ and they pay heavily for it. Usually it's because they don't want to go through the thinking part of marketing. That is, they will hire a company to get them a ton of traffic to their website, only to realize that they are pissing away money because the traffic is not converting. Once they clean up their website, they realize there is no unifying message, and they decide to do the thinking part of marketing last. In the end, this is just a dumb way to approach your marketing.

The Grow! IMS™ reverses this tendency to go to Phase 3 first, and maximizes the return on your marketing investment. First, get clarity on who you are marketing to and where; next, create a website designed to get customers to take action; then, and only then, spend money to drive traffic, attracting customers to your well thought-out message on a well thought-out website.

HOW TO GET THE MOST FROM GROW! IMS™

In order to maximize the effects of the Grow! IMS™, it is important that everyone on your sales and marketing team understands what you are doing and the process with which you're doing it. Don't read this book and then try to implement the system without communicating it to your marketing and sales staff.

You will get the maximum benefit from the Grow! IMS™ if you train everyone on what the system is and how to implement it. It is not a difficult system to understand, but if you try to implement it in a vacuum, you're sure to waste money. Just like in the Air Force, you get the best results if everyone understands the system and how to follow it consistently.

Another way to maximize the Grow! IMS™ is to not go it alone. For each step I have created worksheets and templates you can use to implement the system. I reference these throughout the book and also at the end of each chapter.

These materials are free to download and are updated regularly as we test and improve the Grow! IMS™. The basic steps of the system will never change, but the checklists and procedures will. So be sure to download the worksheets and templates as you implement the system and check back for updates to have the latest resources.

With the basics of the system approach covered, let's do the heavy lifting of the Grow! IMS™ and get clarity on who you are marketing to, where they are located, and how you will connect with them.

CHAPTER SUMMARY AND ACTION CHECKLIST

- Part Two is a step-by-step process of strategizing and implementing The Grow! IMS™. Each chapter is a step to be followed in sequence. Here we will highlight the essential smaller steps or major ideas within each chapter.

- Successful organizations use systems relentlessly. That is why they are successful.

- A system is a series of steps designed to get a specific result.

- The Grow! IMS™ is designed to be followed in the order described to achieve the result of high growth and high profits. Don't stray from the system if you want these results.

- Get all of the checklists and samples for the steps at: www.coalmarch.com/grow-ims

"In trying to please all, he had pleased none."

- Aesop

Chapter 5

Step One:
Establish Marketing Clarity

Maybe it's time for a healthier you. Maybe it's time for you get to the gym to work out and to eat more salads as you know you should. Health and fitness are all the rage now. There are smartphone apps to tell you how many calories there are in the steak you had for dinner. There are smart watches that keep track of how long you've been standing and how many steps you've taken. There are even companies that will deliver an entire week's worth of healthy meals right to your door. All you have to do is go to a website, tell it what diet plan you're on, and voilà, premade meals are delivered the next day. No more horrible, terrible, unhealthy, and outright detestable fast food for you.

Interestingly enough, the fast food industry is desperately trying to overcome the attack from health advocacy groups who publicly shame and vilify them due to the "poison" the fast food industry serves to the general public. It's the fast food industry that's responsible for the obesity problem in America, it's the fast food industry that's responsible for the inhumane treatment of animals, and it's the fast food industry that's to blame for the unprecedented rise in type II diabetes. There's even a documentary film that shows innocent "victims" getting fat from eating highly-processed fast food for 30 straight days. In short, there is a health problem in America and the fast food industry is blamed as public enemy #1.

Make no mistake, the fast food industry has a big PR problem and they know it. This industry is pivoting from menus of high-fat, high-calorie, and highly-processed foods to menus that include more unprocessed foods like fruit and salads. In general, most fast food companies are trying to rebrand to look more like Panera (a brand built on the idea of healthy food) by offering more natural and healthier options.

Seeing its competitors change their menus and marketing, one major fast food company produced a commercial for the 2015 Super Bowl that featured its own "healthy" menu options in the most flamboyant fashion. This commercial generated an unprecedented 2.5 billion impressions before the Super Bowl was ever played. After the Super Bowl, it had over 4 billion impressions. This one single commercial broke every marketing record in terms of impressions both before and after the Super Bowl .

The ad was for Hardee's, and featured the supermodel Charlotte

McKinney walking through a farmers market of fresh vegetables and fruits, explaining how she loves going all natural. It's not what she says that makes the commercial, it's how the commercial took a page from the movie Austin Powers by strategically covering parts of her body with fruits and vegetables to make her appear to be naked. As she walks through the market with guys fawning over her, it's revealed that Charlotte is actually wearing a bikini, so she's not nude, as you were led to believe. Finally, she takes a huge, passionate bite from the new, "all natural" burger from Hardee's. The commercial closes with the words "No-Antibiotics", "No Added Hormones" and "No Steroids" in all capitalized and bold letters and the Hardee's signature slogan, "Hardee's, Eat Like You Mean It," emblazoned across the screen.

So why, in a sea of evidence that consumers are demanding healthier options, would Hardee's try selling a 1,000 calorie burger? Not only that, why would they risk alienating so many viewers by airing an add full of sex, supermodels, and junk food?

CLARITY

Since taking the reins as CEO of CKE Restaurants, Andrew Puzder has staged one of the greatest business comebacks in history. In 1997, when CKE purchased Hardee's, it was a dated and dying brand with only $300 million in sales. Today it's considered to be a premium brand with over 1.2 billion dollars of revenue annually.

Puzder's vision has grown greater profits and revenue for Hardee's by focusing on higher priced, higher quality burgers. Puzder credits the turnaround of Hardee's to this one decision: clearly defining its target customer as young males ages 18-34 and catering exclusively to them.

How committed is Puzder to this demographic? How willing is he to exclude other customer opportunities and even offend others by focusing exclusively on this customer? A recent interview with Entrepreneur Magazine leaves no doubt concerning Puzder's commitment. In the interview, Puzder is quoted as saying:

> *"If you don't complain, I go to the head of marketing and say, 'What's wrong with our ads?' Those complaints aren't necessarily bad for us. What you look at is, you look at sales. And, our sales go up."*

> *"I like our ads. I like beautiful women eating burgers in bikinis. I think it's very American. I used to hear brands take on the personality of the CEO. And I rarely thought that was true, but I think this one, in this case, it kind of did take on my personality."*

> *"Something that other brands are having a problem doing, particularly McDonald's, is*

nobody knows who they are anymore. One thing about us: everybody knows who we are."

Don't misunderstand the point being made here. I am neither an advocate nor antagonist for how Hardee's markets to its target customer. Personally, I no longer fit their demographic, and their ads and their food no longer appeal to me. I also have 4 children, two being daughters, and I wouldn't dream of showing them a single Hardee's commercial.

I am, however, extremely impressed with how much clarity and focus Hardee's has on its target customer. In a time where political correctness and the fear of offending a person or a group is at an all-time high, Hardee's is absolutely fearless in catering to its target customer. Every decision, from menu options to advertising, is a relentless pursuit to give its target consumer exactly what he wants, even if that means establishing a brand that stands for boobs and burgers.

In an industry where overall sales are declining and special interest groups are on the attack, Hardee's has not only insulated itself from the fate of its competitors, but it has thrived despite these challenges. This clarity of who their customer is and what those customers want has given Hardee's the ability to defy industry trends, ignore experts, avoid distractions, and ultimately turn around and grow its business. With clarity, Hardee's understands what it needs to provide and how they should package it. With clarity, Hardee's has a strategy to make decisions quickly and accurately. With clarity, Hardee's only has to focus on one thing - its target customer. Their commitment and clarity has given the company record sales and an authenticity that no other brand in the fast food industry can match, not even Chick-Fil-A.

CLARITY OF THE IDEAL CUSTOMER

Most business owners and leaders avoid clarifying their company's target customer. And if they do, very few are willing to relentlessly focus on that single customer in all aspects of their marketing and fulfilment. Why? Because it's very hard for a business owner to walk away from an opportunity. This reality was once highlighted for me as I was consulting with a marketing software company and I asked "who is your target customer?" Their response was classic "our target customer is anyone with a marketing budget."

This tendency, to want to be all things to all people, ultimately results in your business looking like one big spork. That is, you do a lot of things and you suck at most of them. I hate sporks because they are not a great fork or a great spoon. If you are trying to offer too many services to appeal to more than one target customer, your business is a bonafide spork.

Before spending a single dime on marketing, take the time to critically think through who you want to sell to and what you want to sell them. Doing this will make all your future decisions about the direction of your company and your marketing more straightforward.

Do you have customers you hate, or who hate you? You know who I'm talking about. These are the customers who complain about your prices, complain about your service, complain, complain, complain. It's as if these people have nothing better to do than point out all of the warts on your business. Then there are the customers who, for one reason or another, can't seem to pay their bill on time. And the customers who, no matter how well you do a job, will never think it's good enough.

In all of these cases, there is a mismatch between a customer and a company. Typically, when you have more than 2-3% of customers that fit into this complaining category, it's indicative of one of the following:

- Your service really is bad and you need to address it.
- You have a database of customers who don't fit your company.
- You have both.

If your service is bad, great! Of the options listed above, this is probably the easiest to fix. If your service is good and you are still above the 3% mark, then you have attracted the wrong type of customer to your business. Typically this happens as a result of an acquisition or previous marketing that targeted the wrong demographic.

Getting Hardee's-level clear on who is your ideal customer will have positive ramifications for your entire organization. Think about it: when a customer has money and is a good match for your company, she will pay more for your service, be more satisfied with the service, and appreciate your company more. This results in more sales, greater profits, and better customer service, as they want precisely what you are providing.

START WITH BASIC DEMOGRAPHICS

Demographics are nothing more than markers that quantifiably describe who someone is. Demographics include things such as:

- Age
- Location
- Gender
- Income
- Education
- Occupation
- Ethnicity
- Marital Status
- Number of children

Think about your last purchase. How many of the above demographics influenced that purchasing decision? Chances are at least three of them played a major part in determining the outcome of your purchase decision.

In reality, most service companies should only focus on two core demographics and three-four secondary demographics. For example, if you are a company that provides home services, your two primary demographics are:

- Location - The customer must live in an area you service.
- Income - The customer must be able to afford your service.

The secondary demographics could be:

- Gender - Who makes the buying decision in the home.
- Age - Does the person need the service. (think home health services)
- Number of children.

This is not a process to exclude anyone. It's more about identifying which type of customer would be most positively impacted by using your service.

The idea here is to get absolutely clear on who your target customer is by painting a picture of their life. With this clarity, you can start to deconstruct their habits and their needs. Once you have identified these, you can find ways to integrate into those habits and address the needs of that specific consumer type.

Obtaining third-party demographic data for your service is not that difficult. Most industry associations conduct research to determine the demographics of the people most likely to buy your service. If you haven't explored this option, I'd start there. If your association doesn't provide this type of data, there are several companies that will provide it... for a small fee, of course.

Understand the psychographics of your target

Once you've identified your target customer, it's time to start digging a little deeper. While demographics answer the question of who is buying, psychographics get at the why they buy.

Psychographics identify your target customers:

- Lifestyle
- Behavior
- Interests and hobbies
- Values
- Attitudes
- Personality

Ultimately, psychographics is honing in on and exposing what motivates your target customer to take action and buy. The influential role of emotion on consumer behavior is well documented:

- fMRI neuro-imagery shows that, when evaluating brands, consumers primarily use emotions (personal feelings and experiences) rather than information (brand attributes, features, and facts.)

- Advertising research reveals that their emotional

response to an ad has far greater influence on a consumer's reported intent to buy a product than the ad's content by a factor of three to one.

- Research conducted by the Advertising Research Foundation concluded that the emotion response to "likeability" is the measure most predictive of whether an advertisement will increase a brand's sales.

This all makes sense. What emotion do you think young men feel when they watch a Hardee's commercial? My guess is that it's not hunger; however, that "emotion" carries over to attract hungry young men to their restaurants.

I highly recommend that you don't try to determine this information yourself. We all have what psychologists refer to as projection bias, which is assuming most people think just like us despite our not having any justification for believing this. Using a third party to gather your psychographic data will ensure that you don't introduce this bias to your marketing.

DISCIPLINED FOCUS

Can you say no to a customer who wants to pay you? Seriously?

Years ago, I went through this exact process of defining my target customer and determining their demographics and psychographics. Once I finished the process, I took a good look at my company. I discovered a segment of my current customer base that didn't fit my target customer profile.

Against the advice of my friends and some well meaning industry gurus, I sold off the entire commercial division of our company so that we could focus exclusively on our residential customers. At the time, the sale of this division represented over 20% of my customer base. While I hated the idea of forgoing opportunity on the commercial side of our company, I decided to fully commit to our target customer.

After the sale, I expected our revenue to be flat or slightly higher than the previous year. Turns out I was very wrong. The same year I sold the commercial division, our total revenues grew over 30% from the previous year. The commitment and focus on my target customer not only covered potential loss of revenue due to the sale, but added an additional 30% in new revenue from my target customers. The focus paid off handsomely.

Determining your best type of customer and understanding why they buy is the easy part of the Grow! IMS™. The rubber meets the road when you must tell a customer or an entire customer segment "no." The really hard part of this is to stay focused on your target customer and resist the less desirable ones. Many businesses simply cannot do this, and just like the spork, they are mediocre at best in meeting the needs of their target customer.

The companies that enjoy the fastest growth and greatest profits are the companies that are not afraid to walk away from divergent or less desirable opportunities. These companies have real clarity and a relentless discipline to determine the target customer, focus on their needs, and completely build their business around that target customer. It's this kind of focus that motivates one company to run a counterculture Super Bowl commercial for a 1000 calorie burger while another sells off a division that doesn't fit their strategy any longer.

ONCE YOU'RE CLEAR ON THE TARGET

Once you go through the process of identifying who buys your service and why they buy it, the next step is to determine the best way to position your service in the minds of your target customer. This is exactly what we are going to cover in the next chapter.

CHAPTER SUMMARY AND ACTION CHECKLIST

- Identify the demographics and psychographics of your target market.

- Clearly define your target market based on the best data and information available.

- Focus on your target market with true discipline and don't stray from that focus.

"Always remember that you are absolutely unique. Just like everyone else."

- Margaret Mead

Chapter 6

Step Two:

Define Your Position

Imagine for a moment that you and your competitors are invited to the capital of your state to attend an all-inclusive, no-expense-spared marketing meeting at the most luxurious hotel in the city. The meeting is a barrage of powerpoint presentation after powerpoint presentation on the best strategies to get in front of your target customer. The TV guy goes through his convincing presentation on how many people you can reach with just one commercial. The radio guy shows you just how simple and effective radio can be with just the right jingle. Then there's that direct mail guy, who just last week signed another three companies in your industry because he knows a secret formula to get the phone ringing with just one mailing. The overwhelming message is to do whatever it takes to get in front of your target customer.

After the meeting, you wait with other attendees for an elevator. Everyone is making small talk about the weather and the latest juicy political scandal that all the networks are fawning over. What else are you to do? Let's face it, it's a little awkward to discuss your marketing plans and the new ideas you gleaned from the meeting since the folks there are all your competitors.

As the elevator doors open, you step forward into the almost empty elevator but for a lone guy who's totally preoccupied with his smartphone. As you all crowd in, one of your competitors rambles on about a new and upcoming technological advancement in your industry.

The man in the elevator looks up from his smartphone and asks what seems to be a burning question, "Hey what do you know about the _____ service? I live in _____ (your town) and I need that service."

How ironic! After sitting through two intense days on how to get in front of potential new customers, a prospective customer who just happens to be looking for your exact service in your service area is standing right in front of you. Someone suddenly blurts out, "Hey, well you just ran into the right people here, because we all are in the _____ industry and we all do business in _____."

At this point, things start getting very interesting. The frenzy starts. The obnoxious business owner who always brags about his business pipes up. "You should give me a call. I offer the best service at the most competitive price." Upon hearing that, another owner protests, "actually, our service is the best and our prices are cheaper than his." Then the guy who never speaks at business meetings pipes up with, "we will beat any price that any of these other guys offer."

Bewildered, the customer just stares at the crowd of business owners with a blank look on his face. Finally one owner simply asks, "When do you need this service?" The customer replies, "I need it as soon as possible." The business owner then states, "Great! Our company offers timely appointments and we guarantee you'll be 100% satisfied before we leave. Can we schedule you for 8 AM tomorrow?"

As the elevator door opens and everyone steps forward to exit, the potential customer turns to the business owner who had something specific to offer and says, "That will be great, here's my card with all my information. I'll see you at 8 AM tomorrow."

DO YOU OFFER THE BEST SERVICE FOR THE BEST VALUE?

Why should someone choose to use your company for the service they need? Take some time to think about this question before reading on.

Let me go out on a limb and guess that your answer is one of the following:

- You offer the best service.
- You offer the best value.
- You offer competitive prices.

Since I am already out on a limb, let me go a little further and ask you another question: Have you ever met a business owner who thought his or her service wasn't the best value at the most competitive price?

Most service company owners have a lot of pride and passion invested in their business. Even the slightest insinuation that their service isn't the best would elicit a response akin to telling them that their kids are ugly.

The fact is, every service company owner believes that they offer the best service and the best possible value. I'm willing to bet a steak dinner (and yes I will honor this bet if you call me on it) that if you review all the marketing messages of your competitors and your own messaging too, they all essentially say the same thing:

We offer the best service at the best value.

POSITION - WHY BOTHER?

Once you've identified who purchases your services (demographics) and why they purchase your services (psychographics), it's time to formulate a position that your customers will perceive about your company. But why bother with perceptions?

Let's go back to the elevator scene. The first three business owners said much the same thing; that is, we will give you the best service for the best price. Since the position of each company was essentially the same, the message had no meaning and no emotional connection to the customer. All customers know that each service company believes it offers the best service at the best value.

Unless there's something memorable or unique about your business that directly speaks to the emotions of your target customer, your business is nothing more than noise to them. Research studies show repeatedly that when a customer doesn't see a difference between offers or companies they are 2-3 times less likely to take action. If you offer a service that is not essential, such as lawn care, then the numbers skew more to 5-6 times less likely to take action.

Every sale begins with a customer taking action. If you want to obtain the highest number of actions from every marketing dollar spent, you must have laser focus on your target customer and craft a message that resonates uniquely, compelling them to take action. If you are going with some form of "we offer the best service at the best possible value," you have no position and customers will simply not remember you.

A positioning statement is a clear and concise description of your target customer as well as a compelling picture of how you want that target customer to perceive your brand. Think of a positioning statement as a litmus test that all service and marketing choices must pass in order to be implemented at your company. Every website page, every direct mail piece, every service offering must both align with and support your positioning statement.

There are two main benefits to crafting a clear positioning statement for your company:

- **Complete target customer alignment** - One of the main reasons that Hardee's has been so successful at dramatically growing in a declining industry is that they built their entire company around their target customer. Developing their positioning created the focus to align their menu offerings and advertising directly to the desires of their target customer.

- **Marketing focus** - How many times have you heard the question "tell me about your business?" A positioning statement solidifies who you are, who you serve, and what makes you different. Your sales team knows it, your marketing team knows it and you know it. Without this kind of focus, your marketing will look more like a celebrity marriage -

ever changing but never good.

GUIDELINES FOR YOUR POSITION

So what makes a great positioning statement? How do you go about writing one?

A great positioning statement should generally follow this format:

For *[target customer]*, the *[company name]* service is the *[point of differentiation]* among all service industry and location(s)] because *[reason to believe]*.

For example:

For *upper middle class homeowners located in the Raleigh Metro market*, the *ABC Home Service Company* is the clear choice for a one-stop service company a*mong all service companies in the Raleigh metro areas* because *we offer all of the services these home-owners need to professionally maintain their home*. From lawn care, to pool maintenance even general contracting, ABC Home Service can handle it all.

In the statement, the **target customer** is the demographic that you identified in your research from the last chapter.

The **point of differentiation** describes how your service benefits customers in ways that set you apart from your competitors.

The **service industry and location(s)** is the industry and location in which your company competes.

The **reason to believe** provides compelling evidence for why your target customers should have confidence in your differentiation claims.

To get you started, there is a template on the Coalmarch website that can guide you through this process. See the end of this chapter to download the template.

Keep in mind that your position statement doesn't need to look exactly like this statement; however, it should have the basic elements outlined above. The idea is to ensure that your statement is convincing, meaningful, and important for your target customer. Hint - it should not be best service at best value. That isn't convincing and it's not meaningful.

Here are some further guidelines to help you define an effective positioning statement for your company:

Guideline #1: Make it simple

Your positioning statement should be understandable by a 6th grader. Even if your service company offers complex services, your position should be simple. Keep in mind that the positioning statement is for internal use, not external. The statement brings clarity and focus to everyone who works in your company and everyone (like a outsourced marketing team) who works with your company. Keeping it simple ensures that the message is clear, and everyone understands it and what it means for their role.

Guideline #2: Make it unmistakable

Making your position unmistakable means that your brand is unique to your market. Your position should not overlap with a competitor. If someone in your market already has a specific position, don't try to overpower it or compete with it. This will both confuse your customer and drain your wallet. The reason your target customer should do business with you should be unmistakably yours.

Guideline #3: Make it credible

Being credible builds trust. Pushing the truth doesn't. Here's an example from my recent experience. While checking out at my local grocery store, I noticed a small laminated sign attached to the credit terminal. It said, "if your experience was not the best in the world, please let your cashier know." Every time I read that sign I can't help but chuckle. How can I, or anyone, judge whether my checkout experience is the "best in the world?" I've been to different countries and had equally good experiences with cashiers that didn't even speak my language. Does my local store really believe that they are "best in the world?"

Unless you are an Apple or Coke, trying to occupy an "in the world" position is not believable. If your customers sense that you cannot back the claims of your position, then your target customer will perceive you as untrustworthy and ultimately will not buy from you.

Guideline #4: Make sure you "own" it

As obvious as this may sound, I'm always amazed at how many companies make the mistake of trying to be something that they are not. You've seen these businesses. It's the gun shop that sells liquor, or the hair salon that is also conveniently a travel agency.

Don't take a position that you cannot completely own. If you take a position, own it completely.

If you make promises that you simply cannot back up, your position is essentially that you are a phony, or at the very least, unreliable. Think about it, would you go to a travel agency to get a haircut?

IT'S WORTH THE EFFORT

Years ago, I went through this positioning process with my service company. At the time, I could not for the life of me think of any reason why a customer would want to use my company over my competitors other than the usual: I provide the best service at the best value. I struggled on how to position my company for over three months.

One day, while I was reviewing the psychographics of our target customer, one element stood out: the importance to my customers of having their problem solved as quickly as possible. At the time, no one in my industry offered same-day service. Everyone believed it was impossible to pull off. Whether from pure ignorance or lack of experience, I hastily changed all of our marketing to say:

Same day service, guaranteed!

I had no clue how we were going to pull this off, but it was clearly important to my target customers, and no one else in my market had the guts to do it.

When we launched same-day service, it sucked. My office staff hated me because they couldn't optimize the schedule, and my technicians hated me because their day was no longer predictable (and much longer than before.) On the other hand, sales staff thought the idea was genius. Our sales that first year increased over 48%. Customers loved getting service the same day, and we were the only game in town that could deliver. Taking the position to deliver our service to our customers faster paid off, big time.

We learned many, many hard lessons in that first year after the launch. But as time passed, we refined the concept in our operations and marketing until it became a staple of our business.

Today, I still own this position in all of my markets. Other companies have tried to replicate what we've done, but we own that position. Every piece of marketing, every service offering, and every strategic decision is filtered through our position. Getting clear on our position gave us a greater appeal to our target customer and grew revenues substantially. Without going through the positioning process, as frustrating as it was, we would still be in that elevator talking about how we offer the best service for the best value.

CHAPTER SUMMARY AND ACTION CHECKLIST

- Download the template on the Coalmarch website that will guide you through this process at: www.coalmarch.com/grow-ims

- The best service and the best value is not a position worth taking.

- Establishing your position takes time and thought, but doing it now makes everything that follows easier, more powerful, and you'll get far better results.

"A man is rich in proportion to the number of things he can afford to leave alone."

- Henry David Thoreau

Chapter 7

Step Three:

Create Your Budget

Years ago I attended a business meeting in Denver, CO focusing on the profitability of service companies. At this meeting, I listened to presentations on target operating ratios for our industry along with best practices for how to achieve those operating ratios.

On a walk back from dinner, a good friend and I discussed the challenge of growing a service company fast and profitably. As we went through all the key factors, we hit on the following two areas that must be managed for maximum efficiency:

- Payroll (your people)
- Marketing

We decided that profitability during rapid growth periods is in direct proportion to the level of efficiencies developed in leveraging our people and our marketing. From a high level this is common sense, but as we all know, sometimes what is common sense is not always common practice.

As I thought about our conversation on the flight home from Denver, I realized the following three critical concepts that are foundational to the Grow IMS™:

- Marketing is nothing more than customer acquisition.
- Marketing budgets should be set on efficiency goals, not a percentage of revenue.
- For maximum growth and profit, buy leads - don't buy branding.

MARKETING IS CUSTOMER ACQUISITION

I still remember a particular meeting with my Yellow Pages sales rep all too well. A technician had called in sick, but the work had to get done, so I was the one who did it. It was a Friday afternoon in late December, I was completely filthy, and I was in no way looking forward to this meeting. As I glanced out my office window, I saw the sales rep pull up in her BMW. The cut-off to get into the book for the upcoming year had just passed on Wednesday and she was "trying to do me a favor" by extending the deadline. We exchanged pleasantries, then she immediately dove into her sales presentation.

She obviously had prepared for our meeting. She had call reports, time-on-call reports, and she even had reports on how well my ad was doing compared to my competitors. At the end of the presentation she said, "Donnie, your business is really taking off, look at all of these phone calls you've been getting this year."

She was absolutely correct about my growth. My business had grown over 40% that year and it was all I could do to keep up.

She was absolutely incorrect about the source of the growth. At the time, 38% of my revenue was spent on marketing. The Yellow Pages accounted for 31%, and inbound internet marketing accounted for the other 7%. In terms of lead generation, however, YP only brought in 12% while our inbound efforts brought 88%.

Quite simply, 7% of my marketing budget was producing 88% of my overall leads.

Overspending on marketing that wasn't getting results was, of course, all my fault. Just the previous year, I had tried to cancel my Yellow Page listing, but the sales rep explained that I needed to "get my name out there" and that "many people see your name in the book and then go to the internet to look you up." She argued that in order to be considered a legitimate business, I had to have a listing in the Yellow Pages. Being in the Yellow Pages would help brand my business.

In her mind, tracking only leads and sales from the Yellow Pages was not fair - I had to consider the impact of simply being in the book at all. To her, only looking at sales and leads was short-sighted and unsophisticated. I fell for probably the worst marketing sales trick ever: I allowed the sales rep to change the purpose of my marketing. During that year, I learned that all of this "sophistication" just left me with less money to grow my business and take care of my family.

The **only** purpose of marketing for a service business is to generate sales, nothing else. Not impressions, not phone calls, not reach, nor any other faux measure that takes the focus off the core purpose of marketing - to get you more sales.

If your marketing effort doesn't produce sales, then what's the point? Does it matter that a commercial reaches 8,000,000 people? Does it matter that someone on the radio hears your commercial an average of 8 times a week? Does it matter that others might view you or your business as "unsophisticated" or not "legit"?

At the end of the day, if you don't make a sale, your marketing has failed. Don't let a sales rep convince you that the purpose of marketing has any other goal than generating sales.

BUDGET ON EFFICIENCY, NOT PERCENTAGE OF REVENUE

The percentage-of-revenue method is one of the most common

ways to determine how much to spend on marketing. It makes it easy, as your budget is based on the amount of revenue you plan to generate that year. Though this method is often used, it has major limitations.

Using a percentage-of-revenue approach creates a complete disconnect with your growth and profitability goals. For example, let's say you want to grow by 20% and your industry standard for marketing costs are 8% of revenue. You'd have to hope and pray that 8% of your revenue could produce enough leads to drive an additional 20% of revenue growth. That 8% may or may not be enough to do that.

To create a marketing budget grounded in reality you should use efficiency performance numbers to determine how many leads and sales it will take to achieve your revenue growth goals.

While this may sound a little complicated, it's actually very straight-forward if - and this is a big if - you're tracking your numbers. An entire chapter later in the book is devoted to tracking, so don't worry if you aren't there yet. For now, let's just go through the process of how to build a marketing budget the Grow! IMS™ way.

HOW TO BUILD A GROW! IMS™ BUDGET

The Grow! IMS™ budgeting method is based on knowing your marketing efficiency for both the cost of a sale and the average revenue a sale generates.

Before we get into how to build a Grow IMS™ budget, it's important that we define one very important term that is often debated for hours by business owners. That term is a lead. For our purposes, let's use the following definition:

Lead - *an opportunity to sell a service that you provide.*

If someone emails you and wants a service, it's a lead. If a current customer contacts you for an additional service, it's a lead. If someone calls and requests a service that you don't offer, it's not a lead.

The Grow! IMS™ makes another assumption: leads used for evaluation are paid leads only. Leads generated via an unpaid source (while awesome) should not be counted, as they can mask inefficiencies when you are evaluating the effectiveness of your marketing.

One key number that you absolutely must know is your cost per sale (CPS). This number measures how much money you spend to generate a customer. To determine CPS, you must first determine your cost per lead (CPL) and also know your conversion rate (CR) on those leads.

Once you know CPL and CR, calculating your CPS is very straight-forward. Just use the following equation:

$$CPL = \text{marketing cost} \: / \: \# \text{ of total paid leads}$$

$$CPS = CPL/CR$$

Where:

CPL - *Cost Per Lead (Paid leads)*

CPS - *Cost Per Sale (New sales)*

CR - *Conversion Rate (Leads Won/Total Leads)*

The following example shows you how to calculate your CPS.

Marketing Cost: $100,000

Total Leads: 1500

Won Leads: 600

Conversion Rate: 600 / 1500 = .40

CPL: $100,000 / 1500 = $66.67

CPS: $66.67/.40 = $166.68

* Note: Some calculate CPS by dividing the total marketing costs by the total sales. This can be inaccurate unless you filter out sales that were not generated by marketing. Using the above method ensures that your CPS calculation is based on paid sales only.

Once you've determined your marketing efficiency based on cost, we next determine how well those leads perform at generating revenue.

To determine lead performance, just take the total dollar amount of sales and divide it by the total number of paid leads:

RPL = Revenue Generated / Total number of paid leads

RPS = Revenue Generated / Total number of paid sales

Where:

RPL - *Revenue Per Lead*

RPS - *Revenue Per Sale*

Now that we have all of the efficiency data we need, calculating how much we should budget for marketing is very straight forward. We just take our revenue target and divide that by our average revenue per sale. This gives us the total number of sales we need to make. To get the budget amount, all we need to do is multiply the total number of sales by our cost per sale (CPS).

For example, let's say I want to generate $200,000 in additional revenue in the upcoming year.

Assume:

Target Revenue: $200,000
Revenue Per Sale (RPS): $315
Cost Per Sale (CPS): $135

Target Revenue / RPS = Total # of Sales Needed

$200,000 / $315 = 635 Sales

# of sales * CPS = Budget needed for growth

635 * $135 = $85,725

So that means I will need to budget roughly $86,000 in order to generate an additional $200,000 in revenue.

Note: If you have a recurring service business, you will need to account for lost revenue from cancellations. This can easily be done by adjusting your target revenue to account for the lost revenue and then calculating your budget.

As you can see, this method is a little more involved than just taking a percentage of your revenue; however, it is still straightforward. The key is tracking your marketing so that you know your efficiency numbers. When you track at this level, you'll know if your marketing budget can produce the revenue and profit goals you've set.

If these numbers or formulas seem a little confusing, don't worry. You can download a spreadsheet at the end of this chapter.

Using this spreadsheet, you can forecast your budget based on simple inputs. This spreadsheet will calculate these numbers for you automatically and help you build your marketing budget based on your profit and growth goals.

For maximum growth, buy leads - don't brand

Unless you're Coke, Apple or some other very large company, stay far, far away from putting marketing dollars towards branding. Why? 95% of service companies cannot afford to brand. If you review the research on what it takes to truly build a brand that customers remember & connect with, you'll find that, in most cases, it takes hundreds of millions of dollars in advertising to pull it off.

Branding for small service companies is extremely inefficient. Making sales is not branding's main goal. Stop and re-read that last sentence. That's correct, customer sales is not even a goal of branding. Measuring the effectiveness of branding is not even measured by sales. The goal of branding is to form a place for your company in your customer's mind so he or she will remember you. In the branding world, reach and impressions of your target demographic is all that matters, and most media outlets needed for branding, such as TV and radio, are often prohibitively expensive.

To make the case against branding even stronger, most traditional branding platforms are losing viewers & listeners every month.

In order to grow rapidly and profitably, your company must maximize every dollar of revenue from a sale, and at the same time pay the least amount for that sale. Online marketing does this better than any other channel or platform.

To maximize efficiency, look at all of your marketing channel sources. Rank each source based on both cost per sale (CPS) and revenue per sale (RPS). Once you find the source that's most efficient, dump as much of your marketing budget into that source until you reach your target CPS. If you still have budget left over, then move on to your 2nd most efficient source and max that one out. Continue this way until you either run out of budget or run out of sources. In most cases, you will find that your budget is the first to give. If you are able to move through all of your sources and you still have money that you are looking to spend, then - and only then - would I evaluate using a branding platform such as TV, radio, or re-marketing.

Ultimately, setting your marketing budget the Grow! IMS™ way is a scientific approach using real data. This allows you to grow faster, make more money, and waste less time than your competitors.

Now that you understand how to create a marketing budget based on reality, it's time to put everything we've discussed so far into a comprehensive action plan. In the next chapter, we'll create a short, actionable marketing plan to bring all these pieces together so you will actually use them.

CHAPTER SUMMARY AND ACTION CHECKLIST

- Download and use the marketing budget spreadsheet at: www.coalmarch.com/grow-ims

- Budget on efficiency, not a percentage of revenue.

- Don't begin the next step until you have a marketing budget in place.

"Let our advance worrying become advance thinking and planning."

▬ Winston Churchill

Chapter 8

Step Four:

Create Your Marketing Plan

A couple of years ago, I was preparing for a leadership conference for both of my service companies. I wanted to focus on the value of systems, procedures and checklists. I was thinking about this one day while I was with my daughter, when she asked if we could bake some cookies. Right then, before I could even say yes, I was struck by an idea about how to drive in the importance of systems. I could simply make cookies according to a recipe and relate that back to the importance of having and following procedures. I responded, "Absolutely, but let's make two batches so I can take one to work."

We researched a few different recipes before settling on some peanut butter chocolate chip cookies. While she was preparing them, I reviewed each step of the recipe with her and offered assistance anytime she needed it. As the cookies were baking, they filled the house with a scent that can only be described as a "little bit of heaven."

I have four children, and as you can imagine, the smell brought the other three right down to the kitchen. Once they realized what we'd done, they wanted to make some cookies themselves. Keep in mind that my 3 other children were pretty young to be baking cookies (ages 4, 6 and 8). At that point, my initial idea of making cookies according to a recipe for my meeting, expanded into a more devious plan.

Not wanting to be a "bad" dad, I told the younger kids that they can absolutely make their own cookies, only this time I didn't provide a recipe. My oldest of the three asked "Dad, is it OK if we put cocoa in the cookies?" I responded, "You guys can make these cookies however you want". My go-ahead started a frenzy of baking activity. I watched as they used eggs, salt, cocoa, himalayan salt, lemon juice, and other nefarious ingredients that they thought would make phenomenal cookies. The amazing part about the entire preparation of the dough was not one ingredient got measured.

As they tasted the dough, I could see a few "interesting" looks. Finally one of my boys said, "It will taste better after we cook them." Needless to say, once the ill-fated batch was cooked, no one was interested in those cookies. My youngest said it best: "These cookies taste like dirt." We all laughed about the experience, and

I took both the good batch and the bad batch with me to work Monday morning for our leadership meeting.

Before the meeting started, I said nothing and placed the cookies on the table to see what would happen. As each manager entered the room, the usual comments came in. "Who brought the cookies?" "I love cookies!" I just responded, "Make sure you try each batch, they are both delicious." Maybe that was a little sadistic on my part, but I just loved watching their faces as they tried the batch that the three smaller children prepared without a recipe.

Outside of the pure entertainment value that this exercise brought to our meeting, the cookies taught a "distasteful" lesson of what the end results look like when we just "figure it out" and don't standardize and guide our team. The message was clear (and the cookies proved) that when a known plan is followed, "a little bit of heaven" can be yours. When not, you may end up with the equivalent of dirt. To this day I still get comments on how bad the "dirt" cookies tasted.

WHY HAVE A MARKETING PLAN

When it comes to creating and implementing a marketing plan, what's your approach? Do you just kind of "figure it out" or do you have a recipe that you use and execute regularly?

Logically, we all know that when we make a plan and follow through on that plan, even if it's not a great plan, we get much better results than those who just "figure it out." Just like a recipe, when you have and follow a marketing plan you can extract as much value as possible from the time and money that you invest.

A marketing plan makes all the difference between professional companies that consistently get great results and the companies that seem to go nowhere because they waste money and time on marketing that doesn't work. The Grow! IMS™ is a focused recipe that all but guarantees success - if you simply follow it. Achieving rapid and profitable growth consistently isn't easy, and virtually impossible without a clear and organized marketing plan.

THE GROW! IMS™ MARKETING PLAN

If you haven't already done so, I would highly recommend that you download the Grow! IMS™ marketing template and sample at the end of this chapter.

This template makes creating your plan much easier, as all you need to do is view the sample plan and then fill in the blanks with your company information. Using it makes this process straight-forward and fast. I recommend following along with the sample as you read this chapter.

If you've avoided creating a marketing plan because it seems too complicated or you just don't have time, don't worry. It's very easy to create a Grow! IMS™ marketing plan. You've already completed the most difficult parts in steps 1-3 of the Grow! IMS™ which focus on figuring out who you are and who you sell to.

The marketing plan unifies the efforts of your sales and marketing teams so that they work together to extract the maximum amount of target customers at the lowest possible price.

As we review each section of the plan, refer to the sample Grow! IMS™ marketing plan to see what that section looks like in action.

Vision Statement

The vision statement describes the big picture goal of all your marketing efforts. An easy way to develop your vision is to ask yourself, "if my marketing plan worked perfectly in every way, what would that picture look like?" Your vision statement answers this question, and putting it at the beginning of your plan will clearly communicate to everyone involved in your marketing exactly what the ideal outcome should look like.

Keep the vision statement short and concise. Fight the temptation to write a dissertation of ambiguous and abstract ideals that can't be measured. For example, a clear, concise vision statement may look something like:

ABC service company's vision for 2017 is to capture 23% total market share of residential customers located in the Jacksonville market.

Company Core Values

The core values section of your marketing plan communicates two very important concepts:

- It clearly communicates who you are at your core and what you stand for as a business. Core values provide guidance in the development of your marketing materials, content, and other forms of collateral that communicate to your customers who you are.

- Core values serve as guideposts for the team involved in marketing your business. Core values draw the lines of what is acceptable and what is not. For example, if a core value of your company is honesty, then your team knows that it is unacceptable to stretch the truth in your advertising.

As with the vision statement, this section doesn't need to be long or esoteric. Oftentimes a simple bulleted list with a definition of each value is sufficient.

Target Customer

This section of the plan is exactly as it is titled. Use the target customer worksheet that you completed in Step 1 of the Grow! IMS™ to complete this section of the marketing plan. While you can add all of the data from the target customer worksheet, in most cases it's sufficient to summarize by including the basic demographics and psychographics of your target customer.

Positioning Statement

This section of the plan is exactly as it is titled. Use the positioning worksheet that you completed in Step 2 of the Grow! IMS™ to complete this section of the marketing plan.

Brand Message

It's extremely important to identify and communicate exactly what makes your business unique and different. You've already identified this in your positioning statement. Your brand message explains how you want to communicate that differentiation to your customers.

Customer Segments

Think of customer segments as your target customer in different stages of your business. The main segments that almost all businesses have are:

- **Potential customers** - Target customers who do not yet do business with you.
- **Active customers** - Customers who are actively using your service.
- **Cancelled customers** - Customers who have done business with you and may have a future need for your service.
- **Leads** - Customers who are actively investigating your

services but have not yet committed to your company.

- **Lost leads** - Customers who had a need and inquired about your service but for some reason did not move forward.

There may be more segments of your target customer base, but these are the minimum for any service industry. With customer segments, you can create unique marketing campaigns tailored to that specific segment. For example, you might have a "come back" promotion to your cancelled customers and an upsell campaign to your existing customers.

Marketing Goals

Once you've identified and clearly articulated the ideal outcome of your marketing efforts in your vision statement, it's important to create smaller goals to help you achieve that vision.

While there is an entire subculture on how to create effective goals, we're going to keep it simple and follow only two rules as you create your goals:

- The goal must in some way help achieve your vision. If you set a goal that does not move you towards your vision, it's either a waste of time or it's not a true marketing goal. In either case, it does not belong in the plan.

- The goal must be specific, have a deadline, and have

someone who owns it. With all three of these factors in place, your chances of success skyrocket.

Most importantly, keep in mind that every goal you set must focus on achieving your overall marketing vision.

Marketing Strategy

In the marketing strategy section of your marketing plan, it is time to get down to brass tacks. You'll identify the marketing channels in your advertising program and the costs associated with each one. This section's format is:

Marketing Channel

- **Active Dates** - When the channel will be active. This could be as little as a couple of weeks or the entire year.
- **Target Customer Acquisition Costs** - The target cost per sale (CPS) for this channel.
- **Target Sales** - The total target number of sales for this channel (during the active dates).
- **Campaigns** - The campaigns to be used on the channel.

As with the other sections of the marketing plan, keep this section as clear and concise as you possibly can.

Marketing Budget

This section of the plan is exactly as it is titled. Use the budget worksheet that you completed in Step 3 of the Grow! IMS™ to complete this section of the marketing plan.

Execution Calendar

The execution calendar is a tool you'll use to take all of the information from the first 3 steps and create a simple action plan on how to execute your marketing strategy. It is a cohesive spreadsheet that shows your active campaigns, the channels you're using, and the customer segments you're focused on.

REVIEW YOUR PLAN OFTEN

Even the best of plans are totally worthless if no one knows what's in them or if no one follows them.

Think of writing your marketing plan as half of the process, and consistently reviewing and executing your plan as the other half.

I've worked with many service companies who have marketing plans. The only problem is that they don't know what is written in them, and as a result they don't follow them. As you may have already guessed, the end result of their marketing performance is not much different than the "dirt" cookies that my three young children produced by not following a recipe.

Once you have completed your plan, it's important that you create a process to review your plan at least monthly. This can be a phone call with your marketing company or a regular meeting with your staff. It's of utmost importance that the plan is reviewed by everyone involved in both sales and marketing of your company on a regular, scheduled basis.

CHAPTER SUMMARY AND ACTION CHECKLIST

- Download the Grow! IMS™ marketing template and sample located at: www.coalmarch.com/grow-ims. Use both as you refer back to the chapter.

- Your marketing plan is a repository for some of your previous work as well as some new sections described in the chapter. Read the description, look at the sample and use the template to capture your work.

- Move to the next step, once your marketing plan is complete. But promise yourself that it will not become a document that lives in drawer or a folder on your hard drive. It should be a living document that you will review and add to as you continue working on the system.

"Without mathematics, there's nothing you can do. Everything around you is mathematics. Everything around you is numbers"

— Shakuntala Devi

Chapter 9

Step Five:

Install Your Tracking

This was going to be bad, and I knew it. After months of client dinners, conference receptions, and endless traveling for business, I had gained a substantial amount of weight. Every time I got ready in the morning, my mirror brutally reminded me of this fact. My face was about two times its normal size and my pants looked more like men's yoga pants than business slacks. The real wake up call came when I went to purchase new pants, since none of mine were fitting me. The pants that fit were two sizes larger than what I normally wear. Reality set in. I was fat!

I hadn't stepped on a scale since I'd started seriously gaining, but I needed to know where I stood so I could begin losing weight. While I am not going to share the exact number, let's just say that it was about 40 lbs above my "ideal" weight. I knew it was going to be bad, but I didn't think it was going to be this bad.

Intensity is probably one of my greatest strengths, while at the same time one of my greatest weaknesses. The previous year had seen a series of attempts to use my intensity to lose weight by what could only be described as binge dieting. This "intensity" strategy was not working, and in fact was making me fatter, not leaner. The process typically followed this general pattern:

- Donnie gets tired of being fat
- Donnie decides to get intense and do something extreme to quickly lose all of the fat
- Donnie starts impossible diet that would make Chuck Norris cry
- Donnie deprives himself of anything that tastes good
- Donnie goes to the gym 2 hours a day
- Donnie, sore and hungry, caves to temptation
- Donnie says "I'll start Monday" and meanwhile eats everything in sight
- Donnie goes back to step 1

I had to make a change that worked. I decided that I'd try backing off from the intensity a bit and apply some of the same principles I had learned in business to lose my unwanted weight.

That afternoon, I purchased a FitBit activity tracker and registered on a food tracking website. Next, I integrated the data from my activity tracker with my food tracker app so that every day I could clearly measure what I was eating, how many calories I burned, and how my daily behaviors affected those numbers.

I also decided to tone down the intensity just a little. In fact, my mantra became "progress, not perfection." With my new ability to see the precise difference between the calories I consumed and the calories that I burned, I didn't have to resort to such extreme behaviors. I just needed to focus on the results for the day and burn more calories than I ate.

One year later and 35 pounds lighter, I have learned two very important principles for both business and life:

- **Going extreme isn't always the right strategy** - I will not beat a dead horse on this point, but I'm sure that you, like me, probably figured this one out when you procrastinated and tried to write a term paper in one night. It doesn't work so well for weight loss, either.

- **What gets measured gets done** - We have a saying at my company that goes, "whenever we focus on it, it gets better." The first step to improving anything is to measure where you are presently, then create feedback loops to track your progress.

As it turns out, the key to achieving real and lasting results came down to one simple decision: to get appropriate data and adjust my behavior based on what the data was telling me.

THE FOUNDATIONAL RULE OF PROFITABLE GROWTH

Being successful in marketing your business is no different than losing weight. It's hard, it's a process, and it takes time. And, just like losing weight, you absolutely need feedback systems to give you data so that you can modify your behavior to get better results.

If there ever was a golden rule for profitable growth, it is this:

Track anything and everything associated with customer generation.

Like it or not, your service company is, at its core, a marketing company. Yes, you provide a service to a customer, but when it's all said and done your goal as a business is to obtain and retain customers, nothing else. I'm not devaluing the importance of offering good service, but I am making the point that effective customer acquisition - marketing - is a required core competency for rapid and profitable growth.

If you want to grow your business rapidly and profitably you must become a master marketer. You can bet that rapidly growing companies know their numbers and they know which behaviors drive those numbers.

These companies have feedback systems so they know how and when to make adjustments based on data and logic.

If you fail to get the necessary data to make scientific and logical marketing decisions, then your business will be no different than I was before I got my fitbit and food app. Always trying stuff, putting in intense effort, with mediocre results.

THE ONLY REAL MEASURE OF SUCCESS

Early on, when I was growing my first service company, I contracted with an internet marketing company to manage our website. Our business was growing extremely fast and the majority of my time was spent on managing that growth. Internet marketing was our main driver of growth, but I wasn't spending adequate time focusing on it.

After about 6 months with this company, I started having serious concerns. My internal data showed sales were flat over the previous year, and my leads were flat as well.

The internet marketing company was baffled. All of my key traffic and activity metrics were more than 30% higher than the previous year. Theoretically my sales should've been through the roof.

Thinking that maybe I just needed to be more patient, I decided to wait and see if the traffic numbers would eventually improve my sales. But three months later the trend was the same: high traffic and flat sales.

Digging into my numbers and then theirs, I found the reason for the anomaly. Six months earlier we had installed a "pest library" on our website that described, in detail, different insects. The high-quality content was written by a student earning his PhD in ento-mology. Internet searchers found the content extremely useful, but not for the reason we wanted. Our increase in traffic was due to students with papers to write, not from buyers who wanted to purchase our services.

In marketing, there are countless statistics, aggregations and models you can analyze. You can track customer visits to your website, which TV shows they watch, what they do for entertain-ment, and so many other possibilities of data gathering. Measuring so many statistics and data points means that, at any given time, the chances of at least one of these measurements going up is pretty good. Oftentimes marketing companies will change what is reported to the client based on what is improving. While some of these data points may be helpful, the only real measurement of your marketing success is sales, and nothing else.

INTERNAL TRACKING

I am a trained software engineer. I went to school to study computer science and I spent many years in the profession producing, testing, and debugging software. The software industry is fast-moving and complex, with multi-million dollar enterprises becoming obsolete in a matter of months. Software engineers are often under tremendous pressure to create "new" and "innovative" software that provides more data, more analysis, and more complexity. While super sharp and helpful, software engineers don't run companies.

As a business owner, it's tempting to get caught up in the advanced analytics and key insights that some of these software packages provide. In some instances, these insights are useful to your business and provide a competitive advantage, but most of the time they provide nothing more than a distraction.

I've watched several business owners spend all of their time analyzing data instead of focusing on getting results in key marketing areas; that is, executing their strategy. These owners were more interested in evaluating results then actually getting them. They're like the guy who knows all of the diets and what he needs to do but never actually does anything.

Please don't take me for a Luddite or anti-technology. I'm simply making the point that you should strive for simplicity when obtaining and analyzing your marketing and sales numbers.

Your focus and execution should be based on good data, not over-analysis.

At a minimum, you should be able to answer these questions from your data tracking:

Leads

- How many are you getting?
- How many convert to sales?
- Where are they coming from?
- How much do they cost?

Sales

- How many are you getting?
- Where are they coming from?
- What is the average revenue from a sale?
- How much do they cost?

If you can answer these basic questions, great! You're well on your way. Just be sure to avoid the temptation to spend more time collecting and analyzing data than executing your marketing plan.

If you cannot accurately answer these questions, then start building systems to get this data now. You must do whatever it takes to answer these questions, even if it means getting new software and firing unproductive office employees.

Your goal is to build a solid tracking platform so you can measure the effectiveness of your marketing and sales efforts. Once you have your platform built, you can easily get the essential data that supports you in making informed marketing decisions.

EXTERNAL TRACKING

Once your internal tracking is in place, it's time to get your external tracking in order. External tracking is nothing more than infrastructure to track all of your customer contacts. If you remember only one principle concerning external tracking, it's this:

Don't let anyone contact you without being tracked.

Pulling this off is much more difficult than you might expect. For example, if you have service vehicles, they should be decaled with a call tracking number. Any time someone calls your office, the customer contact information should be obtained. Any time someone emails you, that customer should be tracked. The origin of each and every instance of contact with a customer needs to be captured.

Internal tracking provides the data to measure marketing efficiency, while external tracking provides the data to determine how each marketing channel is performing at generating interest in your business. External tracking is almost exclusively lead tracking.

TRACKING CHECKLIST

As you now know, you must track everything associated with lead and customer generation to grow profitability. Sometimes setting up your internal and external tracking can get a little overwhelming, but it doesn't have to be hard. Download the checklist from the web address at the end of this chapter. This checklist guides you through the process of building your internal and external tracking systems, and provides you with a list of recommended providers for tracking.

CHAPTER SUMMARY AND ACTION CHECKLIST

- Download your tracking checklist at
www.coalmarch.com/grow-ims

- Keep in mind the foundational rule of profitable
growth: track anything and everything
associated with customer generation.

- The only real measurement of your marketing
success is sales, nothing else.

- Don't proceed to the next step until you are
tracking the following:

  - Leads - How many received, how many
  convert to sales, where they come from, and
  how much they cost.

  - Sales - How many, where they come from,
  and average revenue per sale & cost of sale.

"One way to boost our willpower and focus is to manage our distractions instead of letting them manage us."

— Daniel Goleman

Chapter 10

Step Six:

Define Your Sales Funnels

In the 1991 film City Slickers, three friends from Manhattan decide to take a vacation away from their wives. Mitch, played by Billy Crystal, is approaching 40, in the midst of a midlife crisis, and he's absolutely terrified. Mitch and his two friends decide to reignite their masculinity by taking a supervised cattle drive across the Southwest with a gruff cowboy named Curly, played by Jack Palance.

The movie is a hilarious portrayal of Mitch and his friends coming to understand the purpose and meaning of their lives. The crowning scene of the movie is when Mitch and Curly are riding together on the cattle drive and Curly decides to give Mitch his life philosophy.

Curly: *Do you know what the secret of life is?*

Mitch: *No, what?*

Curly: *This.* [holds up one finger]

Mitch: *Your finger?*

Curly: *One thing. Just one thing. You stick to that and everything else don't mean shit.*

Mitch: *That's great. But what's the "one thing?"* [holds up his finger and looks at it]

Curly: [smiles] *That's what you've gotta figure out.*

This exchange became the most famous scene of the movie, and has since been dubbed "Curly's Law."

As it turns out, Curly's advice is probably the best advice that could ever be given to a business owner when developing her website. Most owners waste incredible amounts of money and time on unfocused websites that don't convert. They lose many potential customers because they are trying to be all things to all people.

Is this your website?

How did you create your latest company website? For small business owners, the process usually goes something like this:

- A web designer gets briefed on what you are looking for in your website.
- The designer uses his experience and insight into your market to design a website that resonates with your target customer (assuming you have one defined).
- There's some back and forth between you and the web designer until you reach a design you like.
- The design is built & you launch your new website.

This process results in the standard website that's typically built for most businesses. You probably have a page that talks about your company, another about your services, and a contact form. The site probably has some sort of tracking attached to it and you may even have a pay-per-click advertising campaign to drive more traffic to the site. You believe you have the complete package with everything needed to get great results from your digital marketing platform.

After the launch, you soon discover that the site doesn't produce any more leads than your previous website. For some reason, your new site just can't seem to rank in your target market for the top keywords customers are searching for in your industry.

You spent thousands of dollars on a website built by a professional marketing company that has all of the features and functions of other websites, but for some reason yours simply will not rank. What's the problem?

Maybe the website sucks at attracting visitors

Most business owners and their designers believe that if they build a site, customers will just find it. All they need to do is describe their company and offerings on the site, send the information off to google, maybe buy some traffic with pay-per-click (PPC) advertising or hire a search engine optimization (SEO) company to add some relevant keywords, and watch the traffic roll in.

Assuming that a potential customer will enter your website either from your homepage or from one of your service offering pages is a fundamental flaw in this approach. These pages most often give mixed and weak messages about what they are about and who they are for. We will revisit this concept later in the chapter.

Maybe the website sucks at conversion

Most websites for service companies create an extensive amount of content centered on the idea that someone wants to learn more about their company and their services. This thought process is correct, but the execution is not. They create one single page that lists all of the features and benefits of their services, all of the awards that they've won, their contact information, and maybe even allow the visitor to purchase the service right there online. I mean, at least their mom would be impressed.

This is the same fundamental flaw described previously concerning attraction. When search engines see web pages that have too much content variety, they're identified as a page with many topics, but none of the topics have much strength. This affects the site's visibility to potential customers.

When you need a new pair of running shoes, do you just search "shoes?" It's more likely that you'll search something like "size 11 Nike running shoes." Your potential customers search the same way, looking for something specific. If visitors land on your homepage, and your homepage has a broad message and generic content, the visitor immediately gets the impression that this may not be exactly what they want. The visitor is unable to connect with the content and is likely to move on to the next result in their original search.

If your website follows the pattern above, you're not alone. I would venture to say that over 90% of websites follow this misguided model. Many of the decisions of site design and structure are made based mostly on guesswork, not on solid data analysis. The end result is a mediocre website that produces mediocre results.

YOUR WEBSITE'S "ONE THING"

There are many different website owners and website designers who have different and even sometimes opposing opinions of of a website's purpose.

Some believe a website should just communicate information while others believe that it should help people carry out tasks. Neither of these ideas are necessarily wrong, but as a service company, your website should focus on doing only one thing extremely well:

Getting as many of your target customers as you possibly can to take an action.

As it turns out, Curly's Law is equally applicable to inbound marketing. As a service company, your website's "one thing" is to get people to buy your services, nothing else.

The purpose of your website is not to educate or to "build a community" unless this helps you sell your service. Every web page must focus on moving your target customer forward to a sale.

This may sound like common sense, but I've personally observed business owners wasting thousands of dollars building features and functionality into their website that contribute nothing to sales and offer little value to customers. These elements may be interesting and cool, but they tend to cost you customers and money instead of making sales.

SALES FUNNELS

A sales funnel is a simple & effective way to organize your website to drive actions that lead to sales. It allows you to visualize exactly the steps a customer needs to take to reach your ideal final goal.

Having well-established sales funnels for your website is the key to converting as many visitors as possible into paying customers.

For service companies, goals should be any of the following that apply to your website or company:

- A phone call
- A form submission
- A purchase
- A download

The first step to building a funnel is to put the goal, or the last step, on the bottom. From there, identify the steps a visitor must take in order to get to that goal, and stack them so that step one is at the top.

This model should be the basis of your website design and content. No matter how the customer enters your site, it should be obvious and effortless for them to move through your predetermined funnel.

Optimize your Funnel

A major advantage of building funnels into your website is the ease of spotting and identifying leaks from your funnel. Once you have the funnels for each area of your website defined, all you need to do is model them, analyze the leaks, and then optimize your conversion.

WEBSITE CONVERSION FUNNEL

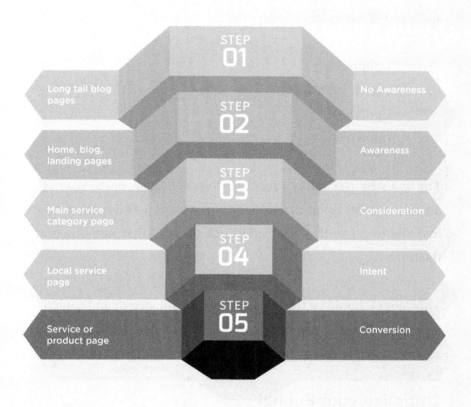

Long tail blog pages — STEP 01 — No Awareness

Home, blog, landing pages — STEP 02 — Awareness

Main service category page — STEP 03 — Consideration

Local service page — STEP 04 — Intent

Service or product page — STEP 05 — Conversion

GROW!™
Inbound Marketing System

Step 1: Model your Funnels

As mentioned in the previous chapter, what gets measured gets managed. When implementing your funnels it's absolutely essential that you model them in your analytics software. You should be able to see how well your target customer is progressing through your funnel and what percentage of them take action. With the modeling data, you're now armed with the infrastructure and information to experiment with page changes and your overall funnel. Without this infrastructure, you're no different than the guys who try to guess as to the best way to build their website.

Step 2: Analyze your Leaks

Once you have your funnels modeled, the next step is to analyze their flow toward your goals. Specifically, you're trying to optimize target customer behavior to see:

- What percentage are proceeding to the next step
- What percentage are jumping out of the funnel to another section of the website
- What percentage are leaving the site all together

To answer these questions there are a few important stats that you must know:

Attrition Rate - The number of users that drop out of your funnel. By analyzing the attrition rate at each step in your funnel, you can work to stop that flow.

Conversion Rate - The number of users that progress to the next step of your funnel. The idea is to measure conversion of your target users from each step in your funnel to your final goal.

Step 3: Optimize your conversions

The process of decreasing attrition and increasing conversion is both an art and a science.

The process is nothing more than:

- Finding your attrition points
- Make a change that you believe will stop the attrition
- Test it
- Repeat

Once your funnels are set up and modeled, experimenting to optimize attraction and conversion through your funnels is an ongoing process. Repeating this process over and over again produces a highly attractive website for your target customer that gives her exactly what she wants right when she wants it, resulting in an abundance of leads.

CHAPTER SUMMARY AND ACTION CHECKLIST

- Your website must focus on the one most important thing: to get as many of your target customers as you possibly can to take an action.

- Use funnels to focus your customers on taking steps towards making a purchase.

- Model your funnels with your analytics software so you can measure results.

- Analyze your leaks. See through analytics where you're losing your customers.

- Optimize your conversions. Identify attrition points, make a change to stop attrition, test, repeat.

"There are risks and costs to action. But they are far less than the long range risks of comfortable inaction."

— John F. Kennedy

Chapter 11

Step Seven:

Design for Conversion

When was the last time you redesigned your website? Before your most recent redesign, how long had it been before you redesigned that one?

In the years that I have been working with business owners in developing a winning online strategy, I've noticed that the majority of them are more caught up in looks than quality.

If you've ever been in a relationship based on looks, you know what I'm talking about. When the relationship starts, the other person can do no wrong. Over time though, you start noticing things that you failed to see before. There's that one toe pointed the wrong way, or the tone your partner takes when they ask you to do something. Over time, the effect of the good looks starts fading and you realize that something has to change in the relationship. Either you have to figure how to make it work, or you have to end it.

Business owners that have a similarly superficial relationship with their website are easy to spot because they all follow the same pattern:

- **Joe sees his competitor's newly launched website.** The competitor's website looks great. It looks fresh, young, and all of the colors seem beautiful and complimentary. The pictures look phenomenal. Joe is quite certain that his competitor is killing it online.

- **Joe looks at his website.** "My website sucks," Joe thinks. In Joe's mind he's falling behind online and his website looks dated. The colors don't really match and the look is just so old. Houston, we have a website problem, and the time is now to rebrand and redesign this old, ragged website.

- **Joe decides to revamp his website**. Knowing full well this is going to be an expensive venture, Joe decides that he needs to start over and build his site from scratch. Everything is wrong with his current site. The content is bad, the design is bad, even the layout is all wrong.
- **Joe hires another web designer**. Joe decides it's

time to get rid of the old company that created his "bad" website and hire a "new" and "better" designer who knows how to build "professional looking" websites. He trusts this new company because he has seen their portfolio of sites and they are absolutely stunning.

- **A new site is built**. The new designer builds the most beautiful and professional website that Joe has ever seen. Joe could not be more proud. The content is crisp, the colors are vivid and the look is so very clean. Now Joe has the most beautiful and professional website in his market and he's happy with his new "girlfriend" website.

- **Joe starts noticing minor issues**. After a few months, Joe's love affair with his new website is over. Now when Joe goes to his website he starts noticing small flaws. The content could be stronger, the colors that he once loved now don't look that great. Joe schedules a conference call with the new designer to get these issues resolved immediately. Changes are made, but Joe still is not super pleased with his website.

- **Competitor launches new website**. Joe returns to step #1.

Joe is essentially stuck in a cycle of spending thousands and thousands of dollars because his definition of what makes a "good website" is not completely accurate. Joe thinks that a good website is one that "looks good" and "looks professional." This definition keeps Joe going from web company to web company repeating the process over and over.

Like relationships, real great web design is a lot deeper than looks. And, just like relationships, they require constant attention.

WHAT IS GOOD WEB DESIGN?

One of the most pervasive and misguided beliefs is that a good website design is a site that looks good. It's not. That's called art. A company or designer who creates pages that look good is not a web designer but an artist. Art is just that, art. Art may or may not have a purpose. Art may or may not have a goal.

Building your website based on art, while beautiful, is not good web design. Good web design is creating a website that has a purpose with empirical goals to achieve. It provides a solution to a problem.

Good web design starts with an understanding of the problem you're trying to solve, both for your customer and your company. In order to solve those problems, you need to ask the following questions:

- Who am I communicating with?
- What problem am I solving for my target customer?
- What is the value to my company of achieving each goal?
- How many specific goals does the site need to have in order to be a success?

These questions form a broader vision of a higher-level marketing strategy, and steps 1-6 of the Grow! IMS™ have helped you to develop the answers.

The problem that most business owners have is that they never take the time to form a strategy, and then they blame the medium when they realize that their marketing isn't working. So they change everything - their website, their web marketing company, sometimes even their marketing person. The problem is not the medium, the website, or even the company. The problem is that they are depending on the medium to be the strategy when in reality the strategy should be focused on identifying target customers and then satisfying the needs of that target customer profitably.

THE GROW! IMS™ CONVERSION STRATEGY

At its core, the Grow! IMS™ is built on the idea of creating a web presence that attracts your target customer to your company and making it as easy as possible for that customer to take action.

Implementing your marketing strategy with your website and the

Grow! IMS™ platform begins with a dogged discipline to get your site to convert as many of your target customers as possible. It is building a medium that does more than just look good, it delivers target customer after target customer. Conversion is the baseline on which this platform is built.

Build a site that can convert and you will attract more customers with less expense. Build a site that is mediocre at converting and you will spend literally hundreds of thousands of dollars bringing traffic to your site, only to lose it because there's no effective sales funnel.

Designing your site so that it converts more target customers is simple if you adhere to three core principles in the Grow! IMS™ conversion strategy.

1. EVERY PAGE IS AN ADVERTISEMENT

Do you have a careers page? What about an about us page? Have you ever thought of these pages like sales funnels, meaning that from these pages your target customer or viewer should take action?

You should view every single page on your site as an advertisement. Advertisements are nothing more than recommendations to do something.

Most web designers and site owners believe that if they have a "contact us" page or a form on the front page then that is sufficient for someone to contact them. It's not. In fact it is woefully inadequate. Attention spans on the web are measured in the milliseconds, and if you make a customer think about what they should be doing next instead of just doing it, visitors will hit the back button just as fast as they clicked on a link to your website.

Viewing every page as an advertisement forces the discipline to think through the purpose of the page and the next step you want the user to take. For a careers page, the next step may be to complete an application, for an about us page the next step may be to learn more about your service. The point here is that if every page on your site has to pass an "advertisement" test then your site will convert much easier and faster.

2. EVERY PAGE FOLLOWS THE 3-STEP MODEL

You only have milliseconds to connect with your target customer when they enter your site. They need to know they're in the right place, or else they'll move on. The 3-step conversion model is designed to quickly grab your target customer's attention and move them into your sales funnel.

Step 1: Get their attention

To get the attention of your target customer, you must have a clear proposition that speaks directly to him on an emotional level. The proposition should be specific, with a clear benefit and immediate gain for the customer.

You don't have to put the entire proposition in the very first header of your page, but the emotion must be there. Use headers further down in the text that allow the target customer to scan your content and get an overall picture of what the page is about. They should be able to find all the basic information they need in under 2 seconds.

Step 2: Get them engaged

Once you have used a clear proposition to emotionally connect with your target customer, get them engaged with your message to create the momentum to pull them down your sales funnel.

Research on funnel momentum shows that there are two essential components that drive engagement as users transition from attention to engagement. Those are:

- Affirm positive signs that your customer wants to see - like reviews and awards
- Resolve their concerns - like fears, doubts, and objections

The point here is that your content should not talk about you or why you are so great. Your content should be engaging by focusing on what the customer wants to see and what the customer is concerned about. Anything more is nothing but noise and will most likely cause the customer to disengage.

Step 3: Call them to action

There is a saying that I use around the office when we are working on copy and site design, inspired by a 1992 hip hop song by Sir Mix-A-Lot:

"I like big buttons and I cannot lie"

That is not quite how the lyrics really go, but it drives home the point that our content must call the customer to action so that they move on to the next step of the funnel. It does not have to be a big button, but those are my personal favorite.

It is human nature to put off action until later. Your site pages should discourage this by calling visitors to action right now. If you cannot convince them to convert now, they are not going to magically convert later. The main things to confirm are:

- That a call to action (CTA) is there
- That your timing is appropriate - that is, don't put a button in the first paragraph of your page
- That you have built momentum - make sure that steps 1 and 2 are all complete
- Create a sense of urgency for the target customer

Every single page on your website should follow this format. While it is obvious that you should do this on your service pages, other pages should be designed this way as well. If they aren't, large leaks will develop in your sales funnel.

For example, every service company should have a careers sales funnel, where the goal is the candidate submitting contact information. Designing this page could be headlined with, "Want to work for a company that appreciates you?" then follow with all of the affirmations for working at your company along with concerns of pay and flexibility. You could close the page with a button that calls them to submit an application. Again, every page is an advertisement, even if the goal isn't a sale.

I cannot overstate the importance of ensuring every page follows this format, even pages you might not expect would need it.

3. Every page is structured as a sales funnel

This last conversion strategy of the Grow! IMS™ system revolves around the idea that every page on your site should feed a specific sales funnel that is modeled and tracked. Once you structure your site, if you have pages that don't fit into any funnel then they should be eliminated completely.

The key is to clearly identify all of your sales funnels and ensure that every page has the purpose and the structure to move the target customer down your funnel.

WITH GROW! IMS™ YOU'RE READY

Because you have already completed steps 1-6 of the Grow! IMS™, you already have a high-level marketing strategy. The information in your strategy makes creating a high-converting website straightforward because you know who you are selling to and why they buy. This is the information that converts target customers. Your website is simply the channel you're using to communicate that message.

CHAPTER SUMMARY AND ACTION CHECKLIST

- Use every page of your website as an advertisement.

- Every page must follow the 3-step Model:

    Get their attention

    Get them engaged

    Call them to action.

- Every page is structured to a sales funnel.

- Download the Grow! IMS™ conversion checklist for your website at:

"You can always count on Americans to do the right thing - after they've tried everything else."

- **Winston Churchill**

Chapter 12

Step Eight:

Create Your SEO Strategy

When I started my first service company, the web was the new wild west. Many companies did not grasp the power of the internet marketing channel, and those who did used every trick in the book to get their company ranked highest for their most valuable keyword searches. Back then, search engine algorithms were very basic, and artificially boosting the ranking of a website was easy.

Armed with a background in computer science and desperate to grow my business fast, I incessantly researched gaps in the system, then exploited them for my business. My competitors lack of understanding of how to leverage the web and my diligence in seeking out high rankings created a perfect environment for my business to rise to the top. In fact, my rankings were so good that my website ranked nationally for some of my target keywords.

After a few years of maintaining the top 3 listings for my target keywords, I think it would be safe to say that I developed a little hubris. I believed my company was invincible online and I would always dominate that marketing channel. I'd been doing it for years. I was the first to dominate on the web and despite the web becoming more popular, none of my competitors could rank organically against us. The only chance my competitors had to get on the first page was to buy pay-per-click (PPC) listings. My company was growing like gangbusters and I never had a problem with getting leads. Life was good and I had golden hands, or so I thought.

What I failed to realize was that in the past few years, Google had started wising up to guys like me who took advantage of their algorithm. In April 2011, Google released a major update to its search algorithm dubbed "Panda." This algorithm update was developed to lower the search rankings of "low quality" and "thin" websites to return better-quality search results. The following year, in addition to Panda, Google also released an update called Penguin. Whereas Panda's focus was to filter out low-quality sites, Penguin was focused on decreasing the ranking of websites that violated Google's Webmaster Guidelines. Feeling like we were untouchable online, I never took the time to read the new guidelines.

In June of 2013, we had a week in which our lead counts dropped almost 20%. While I don't like seeing data like this, sometimes a steep drop-off happens due to the weather. The next week our lead count was off by 28%. The following week our lead count was down 48%. Our lack of leads was crashing the company. I needed to find out what was going on, and fast.

As I stared at the screen, I couldn't have been more horrified and scared. As I searched every major lead-generating keyword, I could feel the fear building inside of me. Now instead of being in the top three listings, in most cases we were not even on the first page. The reason the leads were dropping like a dead man was because my website rankings were literally dying. Now instead of being the most dominant force in our industry online, we were in the nose-bleed section watching with horror as our competitors outranked us in every major category.

As it turns out, our website was violating several of Google's webmaster guidelines and we had simply not taken the time to read them, much less follow them.

There's much more to this story that I am sharing, but the good news is that we recovered. The lesson I learned from this experience is important to remember as we discuss search engine optimization (SEO):

Know and follow search guidelines.

Had we simply spent a fraction of time studying the guidelines that Google updated we would never have been blasted off of the first page of the search listings. The big lesson here is never attempt to outsmart the guy who created and controls the game. Google is that guy!

HOW SEARCH ENGINES WORK

When you think about it, Google and all other search engines are just like you: they need customers. And just like you, Google must provide those customers with an experience that keeps them coming back again and again.

Though Google makes most of its revenue from paid search (to be discussed in the next chapter) the real customer is you and me and all of us as searchers for information. If Google can provide us with precise, clear, and relevant information we will continue to use their service. If they fail, they're gone.

Google is by far the de-facto standard for search. Google has dominated the world of search because its search algorithm indexes and filters information very effectively. While it's beyond the scope of this book to describe in detail how Google's algorithm works, there are a few basics a service company owner needs to understand about search engines and how they produce their organic listings.

In order to provide the searcher with the exact information they are looking for, Google keeps a large database of websites called an index. When you type a query into the search bar, Google searches its database and ranks results back to you based on two key factors: relevance and authority.

Relevance

If you went to Google and typed "best restaurants in Raleigh" and the search engine returned the "best hairdressers in Raleigh," that would be a problem. Who would use a search engine that could not provide relevant information?

Ensuring that the results it returns to an end user are relevant to their search is a fundamental pillar of all search engines.

Of course, with over one billion websites and even more webpages, there are bound to be multiple pages that are relevant to any specific search, so the engines need other criteria for the ranking of their listings.

Authority

Over four million webpages are relevant to a search for "best restaurants in Raleigh." There has to be a way to determine which of these have greater relevance.

In 1996, Sergey Brin and Larry Page, the founders of Google, created a way to predict what users were most likely looking for by ranking the results of relevant topics. They called this concept PageRank (after Larry's last name).

PageRank counts the number of quality links to a page to determine a rough estimate of the website's importance or popularity. The idea is that the more people that link to a specific website, the more likely it is that users who search are looking for that website.

There are many factors that affect these results, but in very simple terms, when you search for "best restaurants in Raleigh," Google takes the four million results and then compares the number of overall links to those websites to determine which of them have the most "authority" on that topic. Those results are then ranked and displayed to the searcher.

THE GROW! IMS™ SEO STRATEGY

The Grow! IMS™ SEO strategy is designed to fill your website with highly relevant pages and quality inbound links, which will signal to search engines that you are the "authority" in your market for your service. The Grow! IMS™ SEO strategy is centered around three core concepts:

- Create a relevant website with landing pages
- Build your website authority by attracting links
- Remove as much spam from your site as possible

Step 1: Create a relevant website

Many web designers and site owners cannot rank well with search engines because they believe that the majority of their traffic enters the website through the home page. This is an incorrect assumption.

The problem with this model is that it's virtually impossible to

TRADITIONAL TRAFFIC MODEL

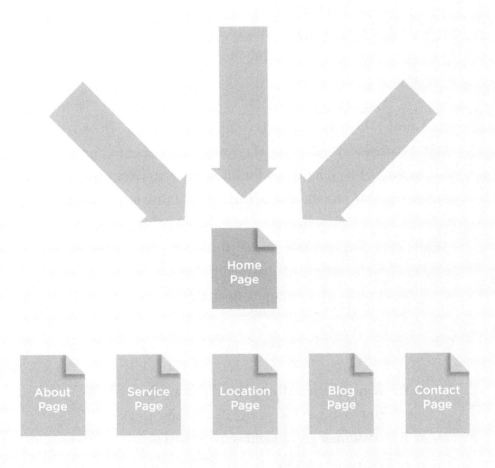

WEBSITE TRAFFIC AND VISITORS

Home Page

About Page

Service Page

Location Page

Blog Page

Contact Page

GROW!™
Inbound Marketing System

be highly relevant for anything. When you design your website to follow the "homepage" model, you unnecessarily create a bottle-neck in which all traffic flows to your single homepage. If that's the only entry to your site, you have to list all of your services and service areas in the same place.

When Google indexes this page, it sees many topics, but none of them carry much strength. This, of course, sends mixed signals to Google, and they subsequently do not recognize authority or relevance in your content.

The Grow! IMS™ site design is completely different. The Grow! IMS™ is based on the concept of creating highly specific and rele-vant individual landing pages for all of your services and all of your service locations. Instead of forcing all of your traffic through the front door, now searchers have hundreds of doors by which to enter your site, and each one is considered highly relevant by Google. These landing pages are then linked to your sales funnel, which drives your target customer to an action.

This design is a win-win because:

- You send Google a strong signal that a page is highly relevant for a specific service in a specific location.
- Your customer gets a highly customized user experience by landing on a page that is exactly matched to what she is looking for (service & location.)

GROW! IMS™ LANDING PAGE MODEL

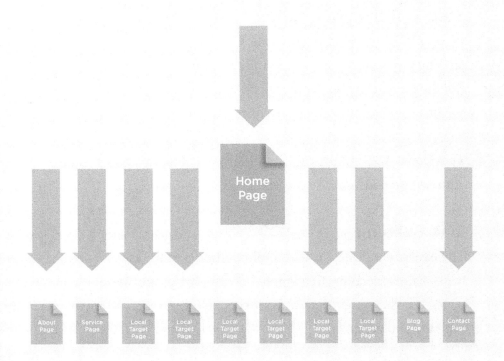

WEBSITE TRAFFIC AND VISITORS

Home Page

About Page — Service Page — Local Target Page — Local Target Page — Local Target Page — Local Target Page — Local Target Page — Local Target Page — Blog Page — Contact Page

This eliminates the bottleneck effect, promoting high rankings and creating a better user experience at the same time.

All of your landing pages should follow the Grow! IMS™ basic SEO guidelines. You can download these at the end of this chapter.

Step 2: Build your authority with links

Once you've redesigned your site to have specific and relevant landing pages, next comes building the authority of your website. Building authority for your site is more of a marathon than a sprint, as it takes time to create content and time to build links.

The Grow! IMS™ uses link building and blog articles to add authority to your site.

Link Building

The easiest and fastest way to build authority is to research all of the social connections that you have within your industry and ask yourself if they might link to your site. Below are some ideas that can help you get links:

- Industry associations
- Vendors (especially marketing vendors such as Angie's List)
- Customers
- Your local news station
- Industry magazines

- Local schools
- Booster clubs
- Causes your company supports

This is not meant to be an exhaustive list. The idea is to build a network of inbound links to your website that signal to Google that you are the authority in your industry and your area.

Blog

Many small business owners obsess over capturing the top keywords in their market. They spend thousands of dollars and countless hours trying to rank for those keywords when in some cases it's all but impossible. While this is an admirable goal, my guess is that you probably don't know this well-established fact:

80% of organic traffic comes from long-tail keywords, and traffic from long-tail keywords carries a much higher conversion rate.

Long-tail traffic refers to the searches that don't involve the top keyword for a particular industry, but variants of that keyword. Going back to our previous example, "best restaurants in Raleigh" is a top search, but there are many, many variants of this search that are much more targeted. Examples such as:

- Best mexican restaurant in Raleigh

- Best restaurant to get chili
- Best dessert restaurant

The long-tail traffic is where most of the search action is happening, and there are endless possibilities to dominate niche markets. Why spend all of your time and money fighting with your competitors over the 20% that's difficult to capture when you can own the 80% with ease?

With a blog, you can write content that not only finds and attracts traffic from the long-tail, but also picks up many quality links in the process. The key is to find niches within your service area that are being underserved and then write quality content so that Google sees that you are the authority in those niches.

For example, ABC Pest Company in Eerie, Indiana might write a summer blog post about mosquito-borne illnesses. By including location-specific language and keywords that follow that long-tail format, someone might Google "preventing Zika in Eerie" and find ABC's page. That searcher is suddenly aware of ABC, may click on a link to learn more about their services, and may even inquire about treatment. They didn't know they were in the market for pest control, and they didn't Google ABC's name, but the blog post lured them to the site, and right into the funnel!

Even better, if you write this content and offer it to a real estate agent, local news source, or even a local blogger in exchange for them linking back to your website, that will add authority and your Google standing will rise.

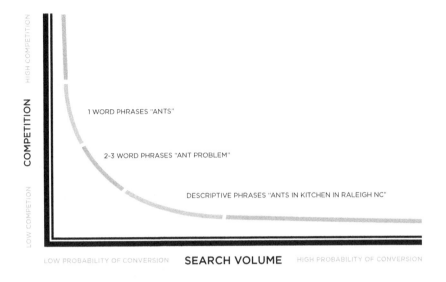

Writing for your blog is very easy once you identify and under-stand your target customer. Armed with the data you collected in the first part of the Grow! IMS™, you can write highly targeted and highly effective content which will attract your target customer to your business. All you need to do is think through common prob-lems, concerns, and needs that your target customer typically has and write content that is relevant to their concerns.

Step 3: Remove as much spam from your site as possible

When we're talking about spam on a website, we're referring to repeating your target keywords on your website, and low-quality, purchased inbound links from other websites.

Since the release of Penguin and Panda, Google has been on a spam witch hunt. The ramifications for having spam on your site are severe and many websites are still feeling the pain from this change.

If you have done all of the steps of the Grow! IMS™ system and your site still will not rank, there is a high probability that your site has a spam penalty associated with it. If you have used some "questionable" techniques in the past to boost the rank of your site, or if you have worked with a company that you suspect may have done that, then you need to contact a professional company to help you remove spam from your domain. With a spam penalty it is virtually impossible to rank well organically.

If you do have spam associated with your domain, get ready for some work. The process to clean up your website profile involves removing and disavowing spam links that point to your website. In some extreme cases, it may even mean creating a new domain name for your business and simply starting over.

If you have spam associated with your website that's affecting results, I strongly urge you to get a professional involved and remove it as fast as you possibly can.

Implementing the Grow! IMS™ SEO step

Of all of the steps in the Grow! IMS™, implementing this step is the most time consuming. While the concept of optimizing your website is fairly straightforward, writing content, requesting links, and constantly researching new niche markets is very time consuming, not to mention ongoing.

Most business owners simply don't have enough time to effectively optimize and tweak their website while running their business well. I highly recommend that you get a professional company involved to help you implement this step of the system. In Chapter 15 I will show you how to screen and pick a high-quality web marketing firm to help you.

If you're technically savvy and feel you do have the time to work this step through consistently, you can download the Grow! IMS™ SEO checklist at the end of this chapter. This checklist walks you through the process we've discussed in this chapter, along with some hints to help you get started.

CHAPTER SUMMARY AND ACTION CHECKLIST

- Download the Grow! IMS™ SEO checklist at: www.coalmarch.com/grow-ims

- Create a relevant website. All of your landing pages should follow the Grow! IMS™ basic SEO guidelines. You can download these guidelines at: www.coalmarch.com/grow-ims

- Build your authority with links.

- Remove as much spam from your site as possible.

- For most owners, hiring a company to execute your SEO strategy is a good use of resources. Don't go it alone unless you have the time and technical expertise to do it effectively.

"There is a very easy way to return from a casino with a small fortune: go there with a large one."

- Jack Yelton

Chapter 13

Step Nine:

Create Your PPC Strategy

Are you a do-it-yourself kind of person? That is, when it comes to home or business projects, do you like to be the one turning the wrench or driving the project?

Growing up, I spent a lot of time with my uncle, who is the quint-essential DIY kind of guy. When something broke, Uncle Norman would always fix it. When something needed painting, he painted it. In general, whatever needed to be done on the farm, whether it was repairing tractors or cutting firewood, Uncle Norman did it. No job was too big and no job was too small. To this day, even though he no longer lives on a farm, my uncle is still a tried and true DIY guy.

For years, I followed in my uncle's footsteps. Usually I did things myself because I had no other options. In other words, I did things myself out of necessity because I had no money.

One day, looking at the roof of my home, I noticed pine straw and leaves bursting from the top of my gutters. They'd been clogged so long that the ground directly under the gutters was eroding. I decided I would clean them out myself. The only problem was that the gutters were located about 36' up above the ground.

I borrowed a ladder from a friend and somehow convinced my father-in-law to assist me. I climbed the 40' ladder, and without a thought of how high up I was, or the possibility of something going wrong, decided that the best way to access the gutters was to stand on the roof.

Everything went fine until it was time to get off of the roof. As I turned my torso to get back on the ladder, my foot completely missed the rung and I slipped off. Luckily, I managed to grasp the gutter with one hand, and another rung of the ladder with the other. With what felt like 5 liters of adrenaline, I pulled myself back onto the ladder and repositioned my feet so that I was no longer dangling 36' in the air.

Once I stabilized myself, I stopped for a minute to compose myself. My legs were shaking so bad from fear, I wasn't sure I could climb back down. Up there on the ladder, I thought to myself, "what the heck am I doing?! If I fall, I can forget flying for the rest of my life, and I will probably lose my company. If I were to kill myself, what would happen to my family?"

I climbed down the ladder very slowly and carefully. I knew then that, even though I could technically clean those gutters myself, I wouldn't choose to try again.

I learned a good lesson from the experience. Just because I know how to do many things, that doesn't mean I should do all of them. And a corollary came to me too: I might not know as much as a professional.

A professional gutter cleaner knows how to properly mount and dismount a ladder. A professional gutter cleaner knows to tie himself off on a roof just in case the unexpected happens. That day on the roof, it became fearfully clear to me that some things demand I pay an expert to handle them. The consequences of me messing it up are just too huge.

I am business owner, not a gutter cleaner. When it comes to operating a company and understanding the finer points of business ownership, I am an expert.

For business owners, getting into online paid advertising is like cleaning your gutters. Yes you can do it, but make sure you have both the time and expertise to do it right.

PPC - YOUR BEST FRENEMY

If your website is not ranking in the top three organic search positions for your most valuable keywords, there's some great news. You can shortcut the process of waiting for your site to organically rank by buying your way to the top. For a fee, you can purchase a sponsored position on the search engine results page (SERP).

Sponsored, or pay-per-click (PPC) advertising is based on the principle of the highest bidder winning. You and your competitors bid on specific target keywords, and the display order is based on who has the highest bid. If a user clicks on a sponsored ad, Google charges you for that click. There are no guarantees of a sale and no refunds. All you buy is a click to your website; getting them to take action and converting them is completely up to you.

Make no mistake, PPC advertising is big business. Google earns billions of dollars annually with 90% of their revenue coming from PPC advertising.

Advertising your company with PPC is like cleaning out your gutters. If you're a small company and your marketing budget is not too big, it can easily be a DIY project. Think of this example as having gutters that are only about 8'-10' off of the ground. Not much potential for injury or damage there. But when your company has a large marketing budget, the time required and the complexity of the operation make the risk of losing money much, much higher. It's akin to climbing that 40' ladder. If you suffer a mishap, it could be quite costly and even cause the death of your company.

I've seen companies waste tens of thousands of dollars per month on PPC advertising that produced little or no results. Oftentimes the owner either doesn't understand what he's doing or simply doesn't have the time to manage the campaigns properly. In other cases, the owner contracted with a company with limited PPC experience and they got poor results.

While anyone can start advertising with Google, it's not automatically a great idea. You have to go through the previous steps in the Grow! IMS™ system to make sure you're ready. Once you've thought through your target customer, designed a message targeted to him and developed your website to convert that target customer, PPC advertising is, in most cases, the most efficient method to grow your business rapidly.

With PPC advertising, you can consistently bring highly qualified traffic to your site from searchers who are specifically looking for your service. If your website is carefully designed to convert them, growing your business online becomes a question of how much you want to spend and how quickly you want to grow.

But don't let all of this opportunity fool you. PPC also has a dark side if you don't know what you're doing. While it's true that PPC done right is by far the most effective, cost-efficient tool to generate customers, but it's also true that you can waste a lot of money, fast. If you target the wrong customers, send traffic to a low-converting page or mismanage your bids, PPC's cost per customer can be 2-3 times more than branding marketing channels like TV and radio.

Given the amount of time and money involved in effectively managing a PPC campaign, I recommend that most business owners not make this a DIY project. As with the gutter cleaning, a lot can go wrong, so you're better off hiring an expert. When you do, make sure you track your cost of sale very closely and make adjustments quickly if the campaigns are not working efficiently.

PPC - WHAT YOU NEED TO KNOW - THE SHORT LIST

Using PPC to grow your business is not difficult or complex. In fact, it will be very easy once you find a vendor who truly knows what they're doing. However, before you hire a company to manage your PPC campaigns, we need to cover the basics so you can manage them effectively.

Run, don't walk, from vendors who own YOUR campaigns

There are currently companies who will take over your PPC campaigns with a proprietary software platform that searches for niche keywords and then bids on them. This software searches within your market and then learns where the deals are for keywords in terms of cost versus conversion. You give these companies a budget and they promise a certain amount of leads per month. But there's a catch, and it's a big one. You don't own or have access to your PPC account or to your campaigns. If you decide to leave one of these companies, you'll have nothing to show for all of the learning that the software did with your money. Once you leave, that's it. Sayonara.

These companies usually provide a layer of reporting between you and the PPC analytics provided by Google. Without access to your account and limitations on reporting, you're unable to see the inefficiencies in campaign management. I've personally observed some of these proprietary softwares buying low-value keywords and then charging a premium to clients. I believe most businesses that operate on this model are shady, if not predatory.

Your first rule when engaging a company to manage your PPC is total and complete transparency. Meaning you own the account and the campaigns. Really good companies are open and transparent and typically only charge a management fee.

If a company is calling you, relentlessly trying to sell you on proprietary software for PPC management, run, don't walk, away from them.

Demand CPC reporting

As described in the tracking chapter, all marketing is nothing more than customer acquisition. The goal of PPC marketing is to maximize your volume of sales while minimizing costs. Your ability to see what's happening with customer acquisition costs is the only way that you can actively manage profitable growth.

Closed-loop marketing is the ability to see which of your marketing efforts actually produce real and tangible customers. While that may sound simple, it's not when you are trying to determine which specific customers clicked which specific PPC ads.

Some software providers offer the ability to integrate your PPC analytics with your customer data to determine which ads produce which customers. As of this writing there are a very limited number of customer relationship management (CRM) software vendors who do this.

If your software allows the integration of PPC analytics and customer data, then you should demand that all of your reporting be displayed in a cost-per-sale context. If your software does not have this capability, then you should demand, at a minimum, a cost-per-conversion (CPC) report. In general, both of these statistics will help you track the effectiveness and efficiency of your PPC marketing.

Tie your PPC campaigns to your landing pages for a one-two punch

One of the most disappointing mistakes I see some business owners make when building their digital marketing program is doing things out of order. The most common mistake is that an owner will want to start generating customers immediately without taking the time to create targeted, conversion-focused landing pages.

When you start a PPC campaign, you want to be sure that your landing pages are just as focused and targeted as your PPC ads. Doing so will increase your conversions from your ads and reduce your overall PPC spending.

Before you spend a dime on PPC advertising, you must have highly targeted landing pages (as mentioned in the previous chapter) that correlate to your highly targeted PPC ads. This way when your target customer clicks on one of your PPC ads, she will be taken to page that aligns with the ad and has exactly what she is looking for.

Control your growth

Imagine for a moment you're driving a sports car. This sports car can go over 200MPH. Would you try to drive the sports car on a mountain road at top speed? Of course not - you'd never make it past the first curve.

PPC advertising is like a sports car for your business. While you can absolutely take your business 200MPH, that doesn't always mean it's a great idea. Your customer experience trumps any amount of marketing you can do, and if you get it wrong, driving your company too fast can do more damage than good.

Give yourself a low benchmark and a high benchmark to keep your gains in check. PPC is a great medium to control both how fast and how slow you want to grow. Your challenge is to maintain this channel so that it benefits, not cripples, your business.

THE GROW! IMS™ PPC STRATEGY

Now that you know the fundamentals of PPC advertising, let's move on to the specific Grow! IMS™ PPC strategy. In general, our system is designed to minimize the amount of time it takes to get phenomenal results while also helping you avoid some of the pitfalls described above.

Step 1: Find an agency that knows what they're doing

The first step in the Grow! IMS™ PPC strategy is to find a company that specializes in PPC campaign management. You'll find that there are a lot of companies that "do" PPC management but very few who really do it well.

When you're deciding on a company, I recommend the following:

- Look for how they report results - If the company does not report CPS/conversion and CPL, eliminate them from your search.

  You want to work with a company that understands your most important goal - customer acquisition - and focuses on getting you the highest quantity of sales at the lowest possible price.

- Look for transparency - As mentioned above, make sure that there is nothing proprietary about what they're offering. If there is, eliminate them from your search.

- Look for results in your industry - At a minimum, a PPC management company should provide you with a couple of companies in your industry to call. If they cannot do that, then eliminate them from your search. When you call, make sure that you ask specific, quantifiable questions. Who cares if they like their rep or if they're nice? You're seeking to determine if the company can deliver results.

If a company makes it through the filters above, there is a high probability that you found a great company to manage your PPC campaign.

Step 2: Build your PPC campaigns to create your traffic

Once you've picked the company, send them your marketing plan along with a sitemap of your website. This does two things:

- It enables them to write highly targeted PPC ads that speak directly to your target customer.
- It enables them to map those highly targeted ads to the appropriate landing pages on your website.

The goal is to create an online experience for your target customers so they see something that speaks to them directly.

When you're building out your campaigns with your vendor, I recommend that you have a meeting to go over in detail the target customer from your marketing plan, and your site map. Doing so allows the vendor to learn about the target customer directly from you, and lets you answer any questions they may have about the plan and site map.

Step 3: Pour as much money as you can into reaching your target CPS

Once you have a great vendor and the website infrastructure to properly configure a highly targeted PPC campaign, the only questions left are: How much? How fast?

How Much?

How much to spend on your PPC marketing really comes down to your profitability goals. I personally keep spending until I reach my target cost per sale (CPS). My CPS varies depending on the time of the year because one of my service companies is a seasonal business.

There is not a good or bad amount to spend. Once you view your marketing results in the context of customer acquisition costs, then the question of how much to spend comes down to how fast you want to grow and how much profit you want to make.

How Fast?

As we mentioned earlier, adjust your speed based on staffing and your ability to keep your customer experience very high. Don't for a moment consider sacrificing your customer experience for growth, as one bad online review could cost you literally hundreds of thousands of dollars in lost opportunity costs. I don't know a single company that can afford that kind of cost per sale.

Step 4: Download the PPC checklist

I have two checklists to help you execute the Grow! IMS™ PPC strategy located at the end of this chapter.

One checklist is for the new DIY owner who may be starting out with a small budget. The other is for larger service companies with marketing budgets over $50K, who use outside PPC agencies. These checklists are a valuable tool to ensure that you maximize both the performance and efficiency of your PPC campaigns.

CHAPTER SUMMARY AND ACTION CHECKLIST

- Find an agency that knows what they're doing. Never use one that owns your campaigns.

- Build Your PPC campaigns to create traffic.

- Pour as much money as you can into reaching your target CPS.

- Download the two PPC checklists at: www. coalmarch.com/grow-ims

"I think that social media has more power than the money they spent."

– Donald Trump

Chapter 14

Step Ten:

Create Your Social Strategy

Have you ever watched a sitcom and wondered why canned laughter is inserted into the scenes? Most people don't like it, and yet sitcoms are notorious for using it. Research shows that when sitcoms roll laugh tracks you not only laugh louder, you also laugh longer. You also perceive that the jokes are funnier than they really are and your experience while watching the show is more pleasurable. Essentially, TV execs are able to manipulate you into having a better overall experience by simply inserting a few laughs, even though the show may actually suck.

Laugh tracks take advantage of what psychologists call a "behavioral trigger." A behavioral trigger makes us behave in a predictable manner when presented with a known stimulus.

We become most susceptible to behavioral triggers when we're rushed or distracted. Usually in these situations we rely on what's known as "single sourcing" to process information and make decisions. Instead of contemplating and looking into the past, projecting into the future, and delving into all of the relevant facts, we simply use a shortcut by looking for a single source of information that has reliably helped us know what was correct in the past. Single sourcing is a surprisingly fast and effective method to make good and quick decisions, and it works... most of the time.

We all have hard-wired behavior patterns, and great marketers (and TV execs) understand them. In his excellent book *The Psychology of Influence*, Robert Cialdini identifies and discusses six common behavior triggers. This book is required reading if you want to build effective and attractive marketing campaigns that connect with your customers on a psychological level. Great marketers know and understand all of the common behavioral triggers as well as their associated action patterns.

When you think about it, marketing is nothing more than communicating a message that resonates with your target customers so they behave (read that to mean buy) the way that you want them to. Some call it manipulation, while others call it influence. No matter what you call it, understanding what your customers want and providing them with the proper triggers to respond to your marketing is the key to building a rock solid social strategy for your company. Ultimately you want to connect with and trigger your target customer, and this takes a lot more than simply opening social media accounts and posting content to them.

The Grow! IMS™ social strategy is centered on three common behavioral triggers: Social proof, liking, and authority.

TRIGGER #1: SOCIAL PROOF - THE MOST POTENT BEHAVIORAL TRIGGER

Let's say you and I were going on a safari together in Africa. Assume that you've never been to Africa before, much less on an actual safari. The trip will last one month, and we'll be crossing rugged terrain. There will be extreme temperatures and lots and lots of rain. Your task is to purchase luggage that can withstand the extreme conditions of this trip.

How would you go about acquiring such a piece of luggage?

If you're like most people, you will research online. Since you've never been to Africa, most likely you'll be a bit uncertain about what to expect. Given your uncertainty, you'll probably want to read about and understand what others have done on an African safari. When it does come time to purchase the luggage, you'll check reviews, read about other's experiences, and then make a purchase decision. Doing this is much quicker than reviewing all of the specific details of the terrain, weather patterns and features of each brand of luggage. Plus, you already have more to do than you can possibly get done, so you want to keep your research time to a minimum.

What you just did in researching luggage is is known as seeking social proof. Social proof, the mother of all behavioral triggers, is where we look to others to see what they've done and then make a decision based on their input.

Leveraging social proof for your service company

Typically, when a prospective customer is looking for a service company, she's unsure who to choose among the many options. Getting your service company to be the clear choice is nothing more than an exercise in manipulating social proof. When your business has strong social proof of performance, the conditions for the desired cued behavior, in this case a purchase, are perfect.

The number one "single source" of information customers uses to make purchases based on social proof are reviews.

Most consumers assume that all professional service companies can perform the service. So as discussed in previous chapters, don't waste your time about being the "best" or a "solution." Spend your time differentiating yourself as the least risky option. What's the best way to do this? Reviews.

When a prospective customer researches your company and sees that you have a history of great customer experiences, they feel that calling you is less risky than calling another company without stellar reviews. A constant flow of positive online reviews serves as a reliable single source of information to trigger the customer to call you, not your competitors.

TRIGGER #2: LIKENESS - LOOKING LIKE YOUR CUSTOMER

Most of us have probably never been interrogated. Of those who have, most would probably never admit it. As part of my professional training in the military, I attended multiple classes on effective interrogation techniques and on how to resist giving substantial information during interrogations.

As you can imagine, there are multiple ways to get information from a person being interrogated. Everything from sleep deprivation to outright physical abuse has been studied and employed. Hollywood is famous for popularizing the idea that you must get the information "by any means necessary." Usually movies depict scenes where the information is forced out of the person being interrogated.

In the real world, effective interrogators use an exact opposite method to get information. It turns out an interrogator who knows how to get people to like them is far more effective than those who interrogate through coercion. Think about it: have you ever done something that you knew you probably shouldn't have, but you did it because you didn't want to disappoint someone you liked? What was it about that person that you just couldn't say no to?

It should come as no surprise that we all have a common trigger to say yes to requests from someone we know and like rather than risk disappointing them. With this behavior trigger, selling services and getting customers to comply with requests becomes easy and simple.

Leveraging likeness for your service company

Salespeople who can't get customers to like them don't last long in the profession. Those who are very good at getting customers to like them are usually the top salespeople in their companies. Top salespeople understand that their success depends on people liking them.

Leveraging likeness for your service company involves understanding one essential principle when it comes to current and past customers:

Your customer must be sold in every single interaction with your company.

Your customers are not bound to do business with your company. Like salespeople, your success is based on your ability to get customers to like and continue to like you. Remember that your customers make a choice about your company each and every time they stroke a check to you or give you their credit card number.

While this seems like common sense, I've sat in meetings where business owners have bragged about "frustrating" their customers and how their customers are "just going to have to get with my program." Such business strategies are about as dumb as the business owners who try to push them.

Leveraging likeness in your service company means connecting with customers through social media and then branding yourself in ways that will appeal to them. Use the psychographics of your target customer to clarify what those messages might look like.

Remember Hardee's? Their target customers are young males, and we all know what they like isn't necessarily what everyone else likes. The company may choose to post a salacious image to appeal specifically to that customer base, even though it might offend other, non-target viewers.

This content is more important than any other aspect of social media, including when or how often you post.

TRIGGER #3: AUTHORITY - BE THE EXPERT

In July of 1961, Stanley Milgram, a psychologist at Yale University, conducted a series of experiments in which he attempted to measure the willingness of study participants to obey an authority figure who instructed them to perform acts conflicting with their personal conscience.

The participants were instructed to administer electric shocks to "volunteers" (who were actually actors) if the volunteers missed questions from a simple exam. The electric shocks were small, but as more questions were missed, the shocks escalated in voltage, to the point of lethality, or so the participants thought. The shocks were not real.

In the experiment, the only thing the participants knew was that Dr. Milgram was in charge. He was the authority, and the participant was expected to comply with that authority's requests, even if it meant shocking another person to death.

The result of his experiment was as sobering as it was startling. The vast majority of participants administered a lethal shock simply because Dr. Milgram wore a white lab coat and told them to do so.

This experiment exposes one of the most common behavioral triggers we respond to when we're not familiar with a topic. When faced with making a decision in an unfamiliar area, we look to an authority or expert to help us make the decision.

Leveraging authority for your service company

Leveraging authority in your service company is not so much an exercise in shocking your employees as it is demonstrating to your potential customers that you are the go-to expert in your service industry.

You cannot become an authority with weak and general claims like "best in Raleigh" or "best at tree care." Offer your customers proof with industry and other third-party awards. These awards should be present in all of your branding to further solidify to your potential customer that you're the trusted authority on your service.

Another technique for leveraging authority is writing authoritative content. Don't be afraid to recommend and suggest action steps in your content and tell your customers what to do. If you follow the funnel step as mentioned earlier in the Grow! IMS™, then this should come naturally, but make sure that your content is not weak in its tone. By adopting a tone of authority in your content, you increase the likelihood of triggering a contact because a customer will trust and respect an authority who guides them to the "right" decision.

THE GROW! IMS™ SOCIAL STRATEGY

The Grow! IMS™ social strategy is designed to use the three core behavioral triggers discussed above to connect with your target customers on an emotional and psychological level. Don't underestimate the power of these techniques. They've been tested heavily in my businesses and those for which I've consulted, and they've consistently produced higher conversions over those who don't use such techniques.

Step #1: Automate positive online review generation

Customer referrals have always been critically important for a service company. These days, customers are using online reviews more and more, rather than the direct person-to-person referrals they used in the past. Focusing on generating an abundance of positive online reviews is like having hundreds of fans that spread your message to thousands and thousands of prospective customers. Reviews are social proof on steroids.

Bright Local, a leading SEO firm, found in their research of online reviews that 80% of consumers give the same amount of trust to online reviews as they do to a personal recommendation. Now we're not talking about the cute reviews that you put on your website or on your branded direct mail piece. We're talking about real customer reviews on third party websites such as Google and Yelp.

In this step you should create a system that delivers a constant flow of positive online reviews. When potential customers are comparing service companies, they're not just looking for positive experiences, they're looking for recent positive experiences with your company. You should have a system in place that ensures a consistent flow of recent reviews.

If you're not actively executing a strategy to leverage social proof in your business, you're literally losing hundreds of thousands, if not millions of dollars in opportunity. Think of it this way. Right now, at this very moment, there's someone in your market seeking your service, and they're completely uncertain who to call. Is your business the obvious choice that others use to solve their problem? If so, they'll call your business. If not, they'll call a competitor who knows how to influence with social proof. Laugh tracks anyone?

Step #2: Use social media to brand your likeability

You cannot be all things to all people, so don't try. Oftentimes I see that many service companies use of social media is completely disjointed and unfocused. Their website reflects a professional service company while their social media posts have a much more casual persona, for example.

It's not uncommon for service companies to hire marketing companies to manage their social media. While this can be a sound business strategy, problems arise if the marketing company is not clear on the persona of your company, or isn't given clear guidelines for what and how to post. Without guidelines, the interests of the person posting on the account can come out. You might see posts about beer fests, wine tasting tours and other useless content that does nothing to strengthen the bond between you and your target customer.

In this step, I recommend that you develop social media guidelines and make certain that your marketing focuses on the content and tone that your target customers find appealing.

Step #3: Create authoritative content

Customers want to buy from people who know what they're doing. Content from your company, whether it's an email or a blog post, should have the tone of an expert who knows what the reader needs to do.

Just like in step #2, a common mistake I see with service companies is producing disjointed or weak content. Oftentimes you'll see emails that say you should "think about" or "consider" a new service. Now that doesn't sound like an authority, does it? Thinking and considering is permissive, not authoritative - "contact us to set up your service now," is. Be bold in your content. Tell the reader what they should do.

In any and all forms of your communication, even your social media posts, be the expert that your customers are looking to follow.

Step #4: Download the social strategy checklist

I have two checklists to help you execute the Grow! IMS™ social strategy located at the end of this chapter. The first is a social media checklist to ensure that your service company has all the basic social media channels covered. The second checklist guides you through the steps of implementing this strategy.

These checklists are a valuable tool for follow up and to ensure that you maximize both the performance and effectiveness of your social strategy for your company.

CHAPTER SUMMARY AND ACTION CHECKLIST

- Focus on the Grow! IMS™ three core behavioral triggers to get best results: social proof, likeness, authority. Other social media participation is optional, these are essential.

- Automate positive online review generation.

- Use social media to brand your likeability.

- Create authoritative content.

- Download the two social strategy checklists at: www.coalmarch.com/grow-ims

"Motivation is what gets you started. Habit is what keeps you going."

— Jim Rohn

Chapter 15

Extending the GROW! IMS™ Framework

The basic idea of this book and the Grow! IMS™ is to give you a sound strategy and framework to accomplish what most service companies believe is impossible; that is, to grow both rapidly and with high profits. With the Grow! IMS™ you can generate an avalanche of customers at a fraction of the cost of acquiring customers through purchasing other companies or using traditional marketing methods. While this system was originally designed for service companies, several other companies in different industries have taken the framework and successfully applied it to generate fast, profitable growth as well. Grow! IMS™ is truly a universal system that can be customized for most businesses.

As you implement the Grow! IMS™ in your company and begin to see results, you'll discover new ways to customize it for better performance. Go for it! Make the system your own.

Personally, I'm constantly seeking to enhance, extend, and improve the framework both for my business and the businesses of my customers. In some ways, the system represents a never-ending pursuit to acquire more customers at the lowest possible price.

As part of the pursuit to improve your results, there are some basic guidelines to follow when implementing and extending the framework to increase the performance of the system.

USE DATA, NOT FEELINGS, TO MAKE DECISIONS

If there ever was a company committed to "big data," it's Target. Target has long collected millions of data points on its customers and then used this data to provide a complete and totally unique, personalized shopping experience.

There is a famous story about just how "targeted" and accurate Target's marketing is through data analysis. In his excellent book, *The Power of Habit*, Charles Duhigg relates a story about an upset dad who complained to his local Target store about the flyers and coupons that they were sending to his teenage daughter.

"My daughter got this in the mail!" he said. "She's still in high school, and you're sending her coupons for baby clothes and cribs? Are you trying to encourage her to get pregnant?"

The store manager quickly apologized for the flyers and promised to contact marketing to let them know of the mistake. Satisfied he had taught the company a lesson, the dad threw the flyer in the trash and left the Target premises.

Two weeks later the dad again called the store manager, only this time his mood and tone were more somber and much less combative.

"I had a talk with my daughter," he said. "It turns out there have been some activities in my house I haven't been completely aware of. She's due in August. I owe you an apology."

The point of this story is that Target's marketing knew that the daughter was pregnant BEFORE the daughter or the dad knew, simply based on aggregating the daughter's shopping patterns. From this data Target not only identified what was going on in her life but they also offered her products that would be appealing to a new mom.

As you implement the Grow! IMS™, make sure that all your decisions are backed by data. Insist on it. This strategy works, but if you implement it with the wrong marketing company or with half-baked data, you won't get the full benefit of the system.

AUTOMATE AS MUCH AS YOU CAN

There is an old saying in computer science that my professors used to quote almost every semester in college:

"Garbage in, garbage out"

- Hundreds of computer science professors

This saying was meant to remind everyone that software programs only work when complete and valid data is fed into them.

While you may not be the most automated office in the industry and you may not have comprehensive technical abilities, don't give up on automating as much as you possibly can in your sales and marketing efforts.

It's a fact that the vast majority of errors in reporting for business or marketing are due to human error. As you implement the Grow! IMS™, look for ways in which you can automate lead and sales data. Also, look for ways you can automate reporting. In short, try to automate all of your tracking and reporting to prevent as much "garbage in" as you can.

Automation provides better tracking, which leads to better reporting, resulting in better decisions. Again, your goal is to prevent the "garbage in."

INTEGRATE AS MUCH AS YOU CAN

Three years ago, our company launched a cross-selling campaign to try and get each current customer to purchase one additional service. The idea was simple. If a customer only purchased one service from us, we'd try to sell them another.

To cross-sell to our current customer base we decided to take a different approach than just calling all of our current customers. After researching the click-through rates from our email campaigns and our response rates from current customers who contacted us for an upcoming service appointment, we determined that a customer who read one of our emails and also had service coming due was five times more likely to buy an additional service than those who were not.

Armed with this data, we launched our campaign. In the first week we sold more additional services than we did the entire summer of the previous year, just calling current customers.

With the key insight of when a customer is most likely to buy, we were able to optimize the cross-selling opportunity. This resulted in higher cross-service sales and less time wasted contacting customers who were not ready to buy.

As you implement the Grow! IMS™, look for opportunities to aggregate your customer data with your marketing data as much as you can. You may not have the resources for the data systems that Target has (neither do I), however, most software packages do offer integrations with other software. Make sure to utilize this as much as possible. Doing so will offer you insights that optimize your marketing efforts and minimize your expenses.

REVISIT YOUR TECHNOLOGY ANNUALLY

At my company, we have an annual meeting totally devoted to new and emerging technologies in our industry. We invite various vendors to our meeting to introduce new products and software that could potentially help us improve our service.

The goal of this meeting isn't to change everything that we're doing, it's more to keep ourselves abreast of all the available options in the marketplace.

Sometimes I'm surprised to see some service company owners wasting thousands of man hours loading data into old software systems. When they started their companies, the software probably worked just fine for their needs, but now, years later, the business is suffering due to the inadequate (and often outdated) software system. I recommend that you develop the habit of reviewing your technology annually and adjusting when new software offers a strategic competitive advantage.

Don't let the tech boat pass you by. Having the right mix of software is a competitive advantage both on the operational side of your business and for marketing. Extending the Grow! IMS™ is no different. Each year you should explore ways in which you can fine tune the system through automation and integration. Building the habit of evaluating technology annually will ensure that you stay on top of current trends and understand what's available for your business.

CHAPTER SUMMARY AND ACTION CHECKLIST

- Here we focus on the important ingredients of implementing and establishing frameworks to ensure that the system operates as designed.

- Use data and not feelings to make decisions.

- Automate as much as you can.

- Integrate as much as you can.

- Revisit your technology annually.

"A good plan violently executed now is better than a perfect plan executed next week."

- George S. Patton

Chapter 16

Implementing GROW! IMS™ Best Practices

A few years ago I gave a presentation at an industry association meeting on how to grow your service company to a million dollars in revenue. There were hundreds of business owners present, including many of my direct competitors.

Instead of giving the same old "rah, rah you can do it" speech, I decided to open up my books and show these owners exactly what the numbers looked like as I grew my own company to a million in revenue, and then to my present multi-million dollar company. My entire presentation was nothing more than me exposing my company. On a large screen, for all to see, I showed a series of reports of the good, the bad, and the outright ugly of all my critical business metrics. I even showed my financial reports. By the time the meeting was over, everyone in the room knew all there was to know about my business based on the numbers.

After the presentation, a friend came up to me and said, "Donnie, thank you so much for showing your numbers. That took some guts! Why did you do that? Aren't you worried about all of your competitors knowing your secrets?" My answer was the same then as it is now. "Knowledge only gets you 10% to your goal, it's what you do with that knowledge that accounts for the other 90%."

Most people go to conferences, read books, and gather all of the information that they need to get better in business, but very few actually put what they learn into practice. You know these people. They're the ones you see at conferences who always seem to have all the answers and they're always optimistic about the upcoming year. Yet, year after year their businesses remain roughly the same.

This story poses a serious question that I'd like you to consider as we come to the end of this book:

Are you a talker or a doer?

A talker is someone who'll read this book and then quickly forget about it once they realize that they must put some effort into implementing the plan. A talker is someone who'll eventually get around to implementing this system... next month, or the beginning of next quarter, or "when things slow down." In the end, a talker will do as he has always done, talk a great game but execute little or nothing.

A doer is the exact opposite. A doer will read this book and start implementing the next day. A doer will do whatever it takes to get traction with the system and get leads flowing into his business. A doer will not look for excuses to delay implementation. A doer will conclude that he needs to start immediately. A doer understands that the longer he waits, the more opportunity is lost, so he works with a purpose. In short, a doer is full of ideas and actions to back them up, not excuses for why to delay.

ORDER IN ALL THINGS

While I know that I stated this earlier in the book, it's so very important that I am repeating it: the Grow! IMS™ is designed to be done in the order it's presented. There is good reasoning behind this.

Section 1 presents the idea that you must be motivated with the proper mindset to grow rapidly and profitably. Your mindset and motivation are the basis of all success; without the right motivation and mindset you'll ultimately fail.

Section 2 covers each step of the Grow! IMS™. Notice how Steps 1-4 have no digital component at all. Before you spend a dime, it's important that your fundamental marketing strategy is clear and well thought out. Skipping the process of identifying your target customer, positioning your company, and creating a marketing budget and plan will result in wasting your time and money.

Steps 5-7 of the Grow! IMS™ is all about getting your digital house in order. These steps come after Steps 1-4 because the ideas and strategy developed in these steps ensure that you create a website guaranteed to convert your target customer.

Steps 8-10 of the Grow! IMS™ are designed to attract your target customers to your website. These steps are the last in The Grow! IMS™ because it makes zero sense to attract customers to a low-converting website not based on a well-conceived marketing strategy.

DO THE HEAVY LIFTING FIRST

If you're out of your element when it comes to marketing, or if you're a little intimidated by the idea of creating a solid marketing strategy, don't let that stop you.

Go to the Coalmarch website, download the samples and templates, and start working. Accept the fact that your first round of this process is not going to be perfect, and that you will make mistakes. That's OK. You'll never have a marketing plan that doesn't change or doesn't need tweaking. Your marketing strategy is a living strategy that needs ongoing attention, at a minimum annually.

As you go through this process, you'll discover what really matters in your marketing. Oftentimes it's the knowledge you gain as you create your marketing strategy that allows you to spot and capitalize on opportunities in the moment to grow your leads and sales.

Spending time and money on attraction or conversion without creating your marketing strategy is like building a house on a shoddy, unsettled foundation. It might stand for awhile, but once a strong storm hits, that house will fall. In the same way, you can waste countless hours and thousands, if not millions, of dollars without the right marketing foundation in place.

If you're committed but still feel like you need help developing your marketing strategy, then reach out to a professional marketing firm for assistance. Any firm that truly knows marketing fundamentals can guide you through the process and help you develop your strategy. However, I'd highly recommend that you do your research before you employ one of these firms, as there are many "talkers" in this industry as well.

HOW TO HIRE A DIGITAL MARKETING COMPANY TO HELP

The Grow! IMS™ is a complete inbound marketing system that you can use to profitability grow your business. While it's true that you can implement the Grow! IMS™ as presented in this book on your own, I don't recommend that you go it alone.

As business owners, we have unbelievable demands on our time and our attention. And it's hard to find the right balance among all the priorities. There are times when we're totally focused on taxes, other times on sales, and still other times on employee issues. It takes clear focus and consistent execution to grow your company both rapidly and profitably with the GROW! IMS™.

I've taught the Grow! IMS™ to hundreds of business owners, and the most successful are those who hire a great team while they remain focused on the big picture. These owners understand that getting lost in the details and spending their time on an area of the business that changes almost daily is a waste of their time. They understand that their job is to have the vision, hire the team, and maintain the focus while a team of experts handles implementation.

While it may sound appealing to just say "ok, I get it, I'll just hire Company X to handle my inbound marketing," it's far trickier than you might expect.

When I started college in the late 90s, the dot com era had arrived and computer technology was white hot, teeming with action and money. It seemed like anyone with an idea and a domain name could get both venture capital and hero status among their friends as a dot com millionaire.

The industry was so hot that after my freshman year, after I declared myself as a computer science major, within three weeks recruiters called me with offers to work as an intern at four different large corporations.

Think about this for a moment. I hadn't taken my first computer science class. I didn't even know how to create a folder on a computer, yet I had four job offers based solely on my intention to study computer science.

Of course, we all know how this bubble ended, with a new phrase added to the urban dictionary: "dot com bomb." The companies that were just getting by on the hype (think toys.com) ended up folding once the bubble burst. Since that time, the industry has returned to normalcy and mostly all that remains are professional companies.

The present world of inbound marketing and SEO services are like the dot com bubble of the late 90s. The demand for these services is so hot right now that if anyone claims they know something about Google they can open up shop and are inundated with customers. There is a bubble of sorts for these types of services. As with all bubbles, there are those who know what they are doing and others who are riding the hype. The challenge is knowing which is which in a crowded market.

Below are some screening checks that you can use to ensure you're not hiring an unqualified inbound marketing company.

Look for a track record

When applying for a job, would you send a potential employer your failures?

When you interview an inbound marketing company, be sure that you are not their "learning customer." Make certain that the company has valid proof that they know what they're doing online and they know your industry.

Don't rely on the "case studies" they send you. Research the company online. Oftentimes you can find clients of an inbound marketing company simply by searching a variant of the phase "website built by _____." Look for websites built by the company for your industry. Once you find these sites, start searching incognito to see how well the "non-case study" clients are ranking for basic industry keyword searches. Also look at how well the content is written and structured. You'll be able to deduce, usually within three sites, if the company is worth your time.

Look for a focus on CPL and CPS

How do they measure your success?

Another important factor to consider when evaluating inbound marketing companies is how they report results back to you. There's a dirty little secret in the inbound marketing industry that many of these "professional" companies use. They constantly shift their focus and the data they report. They will cherry pick keywords that are improving and also use positive signals from analytics to claim that what they're doing is having a positive impact. The fact is that there are so many statistics and variants of statistics that you can make any statement look like it's backed with data. Like my old stat professor used to say, "there are three kinds of lies: lies, damned lies, and statistics."

The point here is that you want to be sure that the company you work with is focused on sales to measure results, nothing else. Not "signals", not impressions, not contacts, not leads. Sales should be the gold standard and the only measurement by which both you and the marketing company determine success.

Look for a team

Would you ask your family doctor to perform brain surgery on you?

The world of inbound marketing literally changes by the minute. Google releases algorithm updates, new platforms launch, new devices are developed and other changes happen all the time. The world of online marketing moves so fast that no single person can possibly keep up with it. The complexity of each platform is becoming increasingly sophisticated as is the knowledge required to implement effectively. Getting the best results on each platform often requires an expert on each specific one.

When you hire someone to manage your inbound marketing, look for companies that have specialists on their staff. They also need someone who will translate your goals to each specialist on the team. Using a team of specialists ensures that:

- You get someone who deeply understands each platform you market on. Oftentimes it's this specialist's knowledge that makes all the difference between a platform working or not.
- You ensure that your company keeps up with changes on each platform because that's the specialist's job. Indeed, in the inbound marketing

world, the challenge is not learning the basics, the challenge is staying relevant.

If you want some help - Coalmarch

If you haven't guessed by now, one of my service companies is an inbound marketing company called Coalmarch. As I was growing my first service company and pushing the boundaries of what I could do online, I went through several inbound marketing companies that were really good at making promises but very light on keeping them. After hiring and firing my fifth company, I'd had enough. I decided to purchase an inbound marketing company with the mission of doing inbound right for service companies. I wanted to create a disciplined company that knows how to get results.

Now, years later, I have accomplished that goal. Coalmarch is a professional inbound marketing company that is process and results driven. Coalmarch is, by design, built around the Grow! IMS™. We specialize in taking service companies with little or no online presence and deliver customers to them at a fraction of the cost of other marketing channels.

If you want help implementing the Grow! IMS™, go to www.coalmarch.com and request a free website evaluation. Of course, any inbound marketing company can help you implement the Grow! IMS™ but it helps to work with a company that's built from the ground up around a tested strategy that gets great results.

Let's stay in touch

My goal in writing this book was to ultimately help you. Now you can do what most business owners just dream about: have both high growth and high profit.

This book describes the exact same system that I've used to grow both of my service companies to the multi-million dollar level, and the same system that I use for our clients. I promise that if you take the time to implement this marketing system, your company will grow. In most cases it will grow faster than you ever thought possible.

I believe it's important to associate with and learn from those who are motivated to succeed. I would love to hear your experience and associate with you as you implement the Grow! IMS™.

email

dshelton@coalmarch.com
(note it may take a little time to respond as I travel frequently)

Twitter

@donnieray3

Facebook

https://www.facebook.com/donnie.r.shelton

CHAPTER SUMMARY AND ACTION CHECKLIST

- Be a doer and not a talker.

- Implement in the order the material is presented. Don't skip steps.

- Do the heavy lifting or strategic work first. Don't seek perfection, part of the process is to review and improve.

- In most cases, business owners don't have the time and focus to implement the entire Grow! IMS™ themselves. If you hire a digital marketing agency, vet them properly through their track record, focus on CPL and CPS, and the expertise of their team.

- If you want help on any and all facets of the system go to www.coalmarch.com and request a free website evaluation. This is an excellent way to get a review of your website and also see how Coalmarch can assist you in implementing the entire Grow! IMS™.

Made in the USA
Columbia, SC
11 September 2018